Cholesterol Control Made Easy

By the same author:

HEARTBEAT: A Complete Guide to Understanding and Preventing Heart Disease

Cholesterol Control Made Easy

*How to Lower Your Cholesterol
for a Healthier Heart*

by Emmanuel Horovitz, M.D.

Foreword by
David H. Blankenhorn, M.D.

Health Trend Publishing, Los Angeles

This book is available at special discounts with bulk purchases for educational or promotional use. For further information, please write:

Health Trend Publishing
P.O. Box 17420
Encino, CA 91416-7420

Publisher's Cataloging-in-Publication Data

Horovitz, Emmanuel.

Cholesterol Control Made Easy: How to Lower
Your Cholesterol for a Healthier Heart

Includes index.

1. Coronary heart disease—Prevention—Popular works.
2. Cholesterol—Health aspects. 3. Low-cholesterol diet.

    616.12   90-80651

ISBN 0-9619329-4-5

9 8 7 6 5 4 3 2 1

To my parents, and to Yael, Michal and Dani

Contents

Acknowledgments

I want to thank Jay Schuster, whose editing, creative abilities, and personal interest in the subject helped immeasurably in the preparation of this book; Dennis Cohen for his special editing talent and his invaluable attention to detail; and Herm Perlmutter for his meticulous review of the final manuscript.

My appreciation also to Lisa Garfield, M.P.H., R.D., a registered dietitian practicing in Tarzana, California. Her review of those portions of the manuscript relating to nutrition, and her assistance in the final review of the charts and tables were most helpful.

Special thanks are due to Terry Sherf, from All Media Services, for her professional advice and especially for her support and encouragement; Dan Poynter for giving of his time and for making many useful suggestions; Marshall Licht and Jason Levine for their assistance with the cover design; Dr. Tony Greenberg for his help with the index; and Eleanor Guzik, R.N., Mary Stephenson R.N., and Chuck Behrman for their review of the manuscript.

I want to thank the people I work with at Kaiser Permanente for their understanding and support, especially Dr. Peter Mahrer.

Finally, I want to express my deep and sincere appreciation to the following individuals who have helped me in so many different ways: Diana Lee Thompson, Eric Shulkind, Karen Shaver, Rachel Grant, and Dr. Alagiriswami Venkatesh.

Foreword

by David H. Blankenhorn, M.D.
Professor of Medicine
Director, Atherosclerosis Research Institute
University of Southern California, School of Medicine

Coronary arteries, the arteries of the heart, were given their name by medieval anatomists because they circle the heart like a corona (the Latin word for crown), to furnish this organ with a vital supply of blood. When these arteries become blocked by the build-up of cholesterol and scar tissue, they leave the heart short of blood, causing coronary heart disease. This turns the heart's "crown" into a crown of thorns.

The great tragedy of coronary heart disease is that it often strikes men and women in the prime of life. The economic cost of coronary heart disease is staggering, possibly 100 billion dollar a year; the human cost is beyond calculation. The good news is that this can be reversed by controlling three key factors—high blood cholesterol, smoking, and high blood pressure.

Cholesterol Control Made Easy offers a step-by-step approach to controlling these factors, so you can reduce your high blood cholesterol and high blood pressure, and quit smoking. It also provides good advice for individuals who need more exercise and are having trouble coping with stress.

Evidence concerning the importance of proper diet in preventing heart disease has been accumulating for almost half a century. First, there were the pioneering studies of Ancel Keys in Europe after World War II. Dr. Keys studied traditional diets of different countries and found that he could predict which countries would have the highest death rates from heart disease based on the kind of foods the people ate.

In this country, the National Diet Heart Study has shown that an average American can continue to eat well while making necessary dietary changes to lower blood cholesterol levels. Also in this country, the Lipid Research Clinics Primary Prevention Trial showed that drug therapy which lowered blood cholesterol levels also reduced the rate of heart attacks.

The most recent link in the diet-blood cholesterol-coronary chain of evidence has been obtained in controlled clinical trials targeted directly at cholesterol and scar tissue in the coronary arteries. This evidence has been obtained through quantitative coronary angiography, a technique producing x-ray pictures which reveal and measure obstructing deposits inside the coronary arteries. Two independent angiographic studies, one in Leiden in the Netherlands and the other in Los Angeles at the University of Southern California, have furnished evidence that diet can determine the formation and fate of cholesterol deposits and scars in the coronary arteries. I recommend readers pay particular attention to Chapters Four through Seven to obtain sound advice on making healthy dietary choices.

There is also excellent advice in Chapter Twelve for those who find that diet alone is not sufficient to control their cholesterol—this can happen even to strict dieters because of inherited family traits. The discussion of calorie dense foods in Chapter Ten will also be helpful to many, both in losing weight, and keeping it off.

Protecting yourself from coronary heart disease is really quite simple, but requires your active participation to achieve that protection. There is no immunizing shot, nor any magic cure. It's up to you to protect yourself. For most people, all it takes is a serious commitment to do it. Reading *Cholesterol Control Made Easy* and following its suggestions is an important first step in achieving a healthier lifestyle and significantly reducing your risk of developing coronary heart disease.

Preface

From all the attention it receives today on television, radio and in newspapers, it's hard to believe that cholesterol was ever an obscure biochemical term. All the major news magazines have featured articles about this newly popular topic, and several books have been written on ways to cure or control high blood cholesterol. Food companies tout the cholesterol-lowering properties of their breakfast cereals, and restaurants now provide special low-fat, low-cholesterol items on their menus.

Yet, despite all this attention, many people are still not sure exactly what cholesterol is, what it does to the body, or what they should be doing about it. And this isn't surprising. For one thing, the bewildering array of articles and theories about cholesterol that appear in the media can make the subject seem complicated. The confusing claims some food companies make about the cholesterol-lowering properties of their products don't help either.

Perhaps you're wondering if there's really a "good" cholesterol, or if a high cholesterol number means a person will get a heart attack. Or, you may want to know how a product whose label claims it has "no cholesterol" can be bad for you.

As a practicing cardiologist, I know how confusing these issues can be to patients. I also know how important it is for people to have accurate information, to minimize the chances that they'll suffer a heart attack, a common result of high blood cholesterol. That's why a few years ago I wrote *Heartbeat: A Complete Guide to Under-standing and Preventing Heart Disease*. The book's purpose was to help heart patients understand the nature of their disease, ask relevant questions, and break some of the communication barriers between them and their doctors. I wanted to educate patients about the various symptoms of heart disease, so that they will seek medical help at an earlier stage, before a major cardiac event, such as a heart attack or bypass surgery, occurred.

Cholesterol Control Made Easy is the next step in the process of making more people aware of the importance a proper diet and regular exercise can play in keeping the heart healthy. Although heart disease remains a major cause of disability and death in this country, the death rate from heart disease has been steadily declining. Evidence indicates that this is due, at least in part, to preventive measures, such as eating a proper diet, quitting smoking, and exercising regularly.

Cholesterol Control Made Easy was written to encourage more people to follow these healthy lifestyle habits. It goes beyond other authoritative books on the subject in several respects. It provides up-to-date, thoroughly researched information, based on the latest guidelines issued by the National Cholesterol Education Program's panel of experts. And it presents this information in readable, clear, easily understood language. In addition, it provides many practical tips and guidelines to encourage you and make it easier for you to lead a healthier lifestyle.

Among the factors that influence your cholesterol level, diet is the one factor you can do something about. For that reason, a major portion of the book deals with nutrition and making the right food choices. As you will see, the emphasis in these chapters is on variety, moderation, and gradual change. But high blood cholesterol is not the only factor that increases the risk of heart disease. Smoking, being overweight, and not exercising can also increase your risk. Each of these factors is discussed, and there are practical suggestions for dealing with them.

I hope *Cholesterol Control Made Easy* will provide answers to the many questions you have, and will motivate you to achieve a better, healthier lifestyle. And remember—it's never too late to change your diet and other habits, improve your health, and increase your chances of living a long and active life.

Cholesterol Control Made Easy

1 Why You Should Care about Cholesterol

You've probably heard a lot about cholesterol lately—how too much of it can affect your health. Just about every week there is a story on the subject in the newspaper or on radio and TV. Perhaps you haven't paid much attention to these stories—after all, you've been feeling just fine.

But now that you've finally had your cholesterol checked and were told it was a bit too high, you are probably wondering what causes blood cholesterol to rise, what a safe level is, and what you can do to bring your level down. In *Cholesterol Control Made Easy*, you'll learn the answers to these and many other questions.

In this chapter, we'll describe what high blood cholesterol can do to your body, especially to your heart. We will also show you that the higher the cholesterol level, the greater the risk of heart disease. If you have high blood cholesterol, however, don't be discouraged—it can be lowered by simply changing the kinds of foods you eat and by following a few simple guidelines.

Cholesterol and Your Heart

Cholesterol is a fat-like substance that is normally present in the blood. Most of the cholesterol is manufactured in the body, primarily in the liver. The rest comes from foods we eat—almost exclusively from animal sources (such as eggs, meat, and dairy products). Blood levels of cholesterol vary among individuals and depend on several factors, including heredity, age, and the type of diet a person eats. Although everyone needs a certain amount of cholesterol, too much can be harmful, because the extra cholesterol can build up on the walls of arteries.

Coronary heart disease, the most common form of heart disease, is caused by the build-up of cholesterol and fat on the inner walls of the coronary arteries (the arteries that feed the heart muscle). The underlying process, called atherosclerosis, involves arteries in the heart, brain, and other parts of the body. During this process, which progresses slowly over a period of years, the lining of the arteries becomes thickened by deposits of fat and cholesterol.

As these deposits, called plaques, continue to build up, the inside of the arteries become narrowed, therefore slowing down the flow of blood to the heart muscle. Usually, this causes no pain or any other symptoms. Over the years, however, when one or more of the coronary arteries become severely clogged with plaques, symptoms eventually occur.

Some patients then may begin having recurrent chest pains (angina) because not enough blood is getting to the heart muscle. Others may suffer permanent damage to an area of the heart muscle (heart attack) when a large coronary artery becomes totally blocked. In some cases, sudden death may be the first and only sign of coronary heart disease.

Despite numerous advances in the treatment of heart disease and two decades of declining death rates for this condition, heart disease remains the leading cause of disability and death in the United States and other industrialized nations (see Heart Facts, next page).

With this incidence of heart disease and the role high blood cholesterol plays in causing it, it is not surprising to learn that one out of every four adults, or about 40 million Americans, have high blood cholesterol (defined as greater than 240 milligrams per deciliter, or mg/dl). More than half have blood cholesterol levels above 200 mg/dl, a figure considered borderline.

Anyone can have high blood cholesterol. In fact, you can be thin and athletic and have a high cholesterol level. The only way to know if your cholesterol is too high is to have a simple blood test. If you haven't had it checked yet, now is the time. Know your cholesterol number! (For more on the cholesterol test, see Chapter 2).

Heart Facts

• In the United States, almost one in two people dies of heart disease and related illnesses. Someone dies from heart disease every 32 seconds.

• As many as 1,500,000 Americans will have a heart attack this year alone, and over a third of them will die from it.

• Heart disease often afflicts people in the prime of life. The average age of men at the time of their first heart attack is in the mid-fifties, for women it is in the mid-sixties.

• The economic cost (health expenditures and lost productivity resulting from disability) attributed to heart disease in 1989 has been estimated at over $100 billion.

The Link between Cholesterol and Heart Disease

Before you consider changing your eating habits and lifestyle, you probably want to be sure that high blood cholesterol is indeed a major cause of heart disease. A look at just a few of the major studies done over the years conclusively proves the link between cholesterol and heart disease.

The Framingham Study

For over forty years, researchers have been studying the health of the people living in Framingham, Massachusetts, paying particular attention to risk factors for heart disease, such as high blood cholesterol, smoking, and high blood pressure. The results of this long-term population study are conclusive: as blood cholesterol level rises, so does the risk of having a heart attack.

This and other studies have shown that blood cholesterol levels can predict a person's chances of developing coronary heart disease. These studies have consistently shown that the rates of coronary

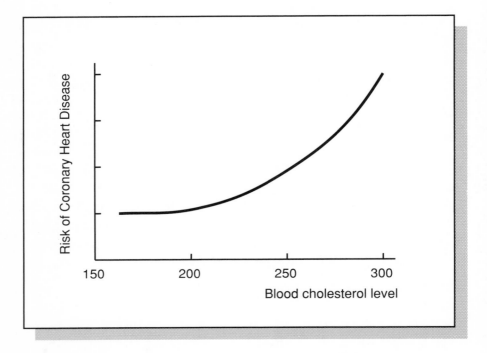

Chart 1. The risk of coronary heart disease rises with increasing blood cholesterol levels. The risk increases rapidly as levels rise above 200 mg/dl.

heart disease remain relatively constant for cholesterol levels up to the 200 mg/dl range. As blood cholesterol levels rise above this range, the risk increases significantly. (See chart 1).

For example, if the cholesterol level goes from 200 mg/dl to 250 mg/dl, the risk of having a heart attack doubles. Then, if it goes from 250 mg/dl to 300 mg/dl, the risk doubles again. Thus, a person with a cholesterol level of 300 mg/dl has four times the risk of having a heart attack than a person with a level of only 200 mg/dl.

Comparisons between Countries

People living in countries with diets rich in animal fat and cholesterol have a significantly greater incidence of atherosclerosis and heart disease than people living in countries where diets are relatively low in fat and cholesterol.

For example, people living in Finland were found to have the fattiest diet of all. Not coincidentally, they also had the highest concentrations of cholesterol in their blood and the highest incidence of heart disease. The United States, which came in second in terms of fat and cholesterol in the diet, was also second in the rate of heart disease.

On the other hand, in Japan, where people eat a diet typically low in animal fats and cholesterol, there is a low incidence of heart disease. It is interesting to note, however, that when Japanese migrate to the United States and adopt the typical American diet, the incidence of heart disease goes up dramatically—to four times what it had been in their native country. Not surprisingly, the concentration of cholesterol found in their blood after relocating here has been shown to increase in direct proportion to the amount of animal fat and cholesterol in their diet.

Lowering Cholesterol Can Prevent Heart Disease

We have just seen how strong the link is between elevated blood cholesterol and the incidence of coronary heart disease. The question you may be asking then is whether lowering blood cholesterol (by diet or medications) can indeed reduce the risk. This issue has been addressed in several large-scale clinical studies, two of which are described below.

The Coronary Primary Prevention Trial

The study included two groups of healthy men with identical risk of heart disease. At the beginning of the study, both groups had high blood cholesterol levels averaging 300 mg/dl, a figure well above the desirable levels of 200 mg/dl. Both groups followed a diet low in animal fat and cholesterol. In addition, one group received a medication (cholestyramine) that lowered their blood cholesterol levels while the other group received a placebo, that is, a substance that looked and tasted like the real medication but had no blood cholesterol-lowering effect.

At the end of a ten-year period, there was a definite difference in the rate of coronary heart disease between the two groups. The group that used the real medication had a lower average blood cholesterol level and a lower rate of fatal and nonfatal heart attacks than the group that received the placebo.

Interestingly, the study showed that for each 1% reduction in blood cholesterol levels, there was a 2% reduction in the number of heart attacks. Therefore, even a 10-15% reduction in cholesterol levels, which can result from changes in the diet, could reduce the risk of having a heart attack by 20-30%.

The Cholesterol-Lowering Atherosclerosis Study

In a study of patients who had had a previous coronary bypass operation (which is designed to create a detour that lets blood go around blockages in the coronary arteries), substantial lowering of blood cholesterol led to a slowing of the formation of fatty deposits in the coronary arteries.

At the beginning of the study, all patients had blockages (documented by an angiogram—a test that provides a picture of the coronary arteries) that were severe enough to require an operation. Among those who lowered their blood cholesterol significantly, there were fewer new fatty deposits and fewer increases in the size of existing deposits. In addition, in a number of patients there was some regression (shrinkage) of the fatty deposits.

You Can Control Your Cholesterol

Your cholesterol level is influenced by the amount and kinds of fats you eat. For example, diets high in saturated fats and cholesterol (such as butter, dairy products, and fatty cuts of meat) tend to raise blood cholesterol. Diets low in saturated fats and cholesterol, on the other hand, tend to keep it low.

You can lower your cholesterol by changing the kinds of foods you eat. Cutting back on foods rich in saturated fats and cholesterol is the most effective way to do that. Another way is to increase the

> **Remember:**
>
> If your cholesterol level is too high, lowering it will reduce your risk. The lower your cholesterol level, the less chance you have of developing heart disease.

amount of foods rich in complex carbohydrates (such as bread, cereals, pasta, and "starchy" vegetables) and soluble fiber (such as oat bran, dry beans, and some fruits and vegetables).

You'll have to make some changes in your eating habits in order to lower your cholesterol. Fortunately, however, you won't have to give up all foods that contain saturated fat and cholesterol. You'll learn how to change your diet without taking drastic measures and without depriving yourself of the pleasures of eating. You'll also learn how to choose the right foods, how to read nutrition labels, and how to use food tables. And soon you'll be shopping for different foods, preparing some foods differently, even modifying your choices at restaurants and parties.

By making changes in your diet and monitoring your progress with regular checkups, you can lower your cholesterol and reduce your risk of heart disease. Generally, your cholesterol level should begin to drop 3 or 4 weeks after having started your new diet. Over time, you'll be able to reduce your cholesterol level by 30 to 60 "points" (mg/dl), or even more.

Though high blood cholesterol is such an important factor in causing heart disease, it is not the only factor. Other conditions and habits, such as smoking and high blood pressure, also increase your risk. Therefore, if you want to keep your heart healthy, you may have to make some other changes in your lifestyle, such as quitting smoking and getting your blood pressure under control. If you are overweight, losing pounds will also help reduce your risk. Regular exercise will help you lose those extra pounds while at the same time improving your health and vitality.

Remember:

It's never too late (or too soon) to begin to lower your cholesterol. Don't wait until you have a heart attack or a coronary bypass operation before making the necessary adjustments. There is no better time for you to start a new, healthier lifestyle than today!

By beginning this book you've already taken the first step toward improved health. The rewards to be gained by following the *Cholesterol Control Made Easy* program are great. You'll learn how to make the right food choices, how to control your weight without feeling deprived, and how to reduce your risk of having a heart attack. And most important, by taking these steps, you'll increase your chances of living a long, active, and healthy life.

2 Your Cholesterol Number: How High Is Too High?

In the previous chapter we discussed the link between high blood cholesterol and the risk of heart disease. In particular, you've learned that the higher the cholesterol level, the greater the risk of developing heart disease.

In this chapter you'll learn more about blood cholesterol and the factors that influence its level. You'll learn about the cholesterol test and the meaning of the cholesterol number. Knowing about the test and being aware of your own cholesterol number, you'll have a better understanding of your risk and, perhaps more important, you'll find out what steps you can take to reduce that risk.

About Cholesterol, Triglycerides, and Lipoproteins

As we've seen, *cholesterol* is a fat-like, soft, waxy substance that is normally present in the blood. Our body needs cholesterol for making cell walls, and as a building block for producing hormones (substances that regulate vital body functions and processes) and bile acids (substances secreted by the liver to aid in digestion).

The cholesterol in the body has two sources. Most of it is manufactured in the liver, then sent through the bloodstream to cells throughout the body. The rest of the cholesterol comes from the diet, almost exclusively from animal sources (such as eggs, meat, chicken, fish, milk, and dairy products). Even if you ate foods containing no cholesterol, your body would make enough for its needs on its own.

Triglycerides are the most common type of fat found in fatty tissues. Triglycerides represent a storage form of fat, and they can be broken down to produce energy. As with cholesterol, the triglycerides have two origins: some are made in the body and the rest come from the diet. The liver converts excess calories (from fatty foods, sugars, and alcohol) into triglycerides, which are transported into the blood, and then to fat cells in various parts of the body. Unlike cholesterol, triglycerides are found in vegetable as well as animal fats.

Fats do not dissolve in water ("fat and water don't mix"). For this reason, cholesterol and triglycerides do not circulate freely in the blood, which is mostly water. Rather, they are carried in the form of tiny, round particles or packages, called *lipoproteins*, that combine lipids (fats) and proteins. Lipoproteins are formed in the liver and carry cholesterol and triglycerides through the body.

Depending on their composition, lipoproteins are classified into several types, including the low density lipoproteins (LDLs) and high density lipoproteins (HDLs). The LDLs are the major carriers of cholesterol in the blood. They are responsible for transporting cholesterol from the liver to the body cells and can cause build-up of fatty plaques in the lining of the arteries— they are "bad" for us. The HDLs, on the other hand, protect the arteries against build-up of fatty plaques, and are considered "good." (For more on "good" and "bad" cholesterol, see Chapter 3).

The Factors That Influence Your Cholesterol Level

There are a number of factors that influence your cholesterol level. The first of these is the *type of diet* you eat. Generally, foods high in saturated fats (such as butter, dairy products, and fatty cuts of meat) and cholesterol (such as egg yolks and organ meats) tend to raise your blood cholesterol level, whereas foods rich in complex carbohydrates and fiber (bread, cereals, pasta, vegetables, and fruits) tend to keep it low. In countries with a high standard of living where diets rich in animal fats are common, the levels of blood cholesterol are generally higher and the risk of heart disease is greater than in poorer countries where vegetarian-type diets prevail.

Age and *gender* also influence blood cholesterol levels. In the United States, cholesterol levels in men and women normally start to rise at about age 20. In men, the average blood cholesterol reaches its highest level around age 50 and then levels off. The average cholesterol level in women prior to menopause (45 to 55 years) is lower than that of men of the same age. After menopause, however, it usually increases to a level higher than that of men. Use of oral contraceptives can increase the cholesterol level in some women, as can pregnancy.

Heredity can also affect blood cholesterol levels. Normally, the cholesterol-rich LDLs are removed from the blood by specific structures located on the cell surfaces, called LDL receptors. Once inside the cells, cholesterol from the LDL particles is processed and eliminated. The number and level of activity of these LDL receptors are determined by the genetic makeup of a person.

LDL particles will remain in the bloodstream for varying periods of time, depending on how numerous and active the LDL receptors are. This explains why some people tend to have a significant change in their cholesterol level in response to dietary changes, whereas others don't.

About 1 in every 500 adults has an inherited tendency to have very high blood cholesterol levels, exceeding 300 mg/dl. In this genetic disorder, termed familial hypercholesterolemia, the person has a defective gene for the LDL receptor. As a result, LDL receptors are less numerous and not as active. Affected individuals sometimes develop coronary heart disease (angina and heart attacks) in their thirties or forties.

Remember:

Among the factors that influence your cholesterol level (diet, age, gender, and heredity), diet is the one factor you can do something about. Therefore, if you have high blood cholesterol, changing your diet is the most important step you can take.

The Cholesterol Test

You should have your blood cholesterol checked at least once every five years, more frequently if it is elevated. The most practical way is to have your cholesterol level checked periodically as part of your regular medical examination. For the test, a sample is obtained by drawing blood from a vein in your arm. The sample is then sent to the laboratory for analysis. The result is expressed in milligrams per deciliter (mg/dl), a measure that represents the concentration of cholesterol in the blood.

In screening programs, blood cholesterol levels are usually measured using a drop of blood obtained by pricking a finger, an almost painless procedure. The tiny "fingerstick" blood sample is then analyzed by a portable machine that gives a cholesterol value within minutes. These screening methods usually provide only approximate values, and the results may vary. Therefore, if your cholesterol values are abnormal, they probably should be rechecked by having your doctor take another sample.

Total cholesterol can be measured at any time of the day, whether or not you've just eaten, since total cholesterol levels change very little after a meal. However, if you are scheduled to have a *lipid profile* (that is, including LDL, HDL, and triglyceride levels—see Chapter 3), then you should be fasting (except for water

---

Remember:

• The only way for you to know if your cholesterol is too high is to have it checked. If you haven't had your cholesterol checked yet, now is the time. Ask for the actual number (and not just if it's "normal").

• You should have your cholesterol checked at least once every five years, more frequently if it's elevated. The most practical way is to have it checked periodically as part as your regular physical examination.

or black coffee) for at least 12 hours before the test. It may be convenient, for example, to eat your last meal in the evening, and have your test the next day before breakfast.

To obtain reliable cholesterol levels, you should follow your ordinary eating habits and be in your usual state of health. If you are acutely ill or are participating in a weight-loss program, the results obtained may not represent your usual cholesterol levels. For the same reason, if you are a woman and pregnant, or if you've had a heart attack within the past three months, your cholesterol test should be postponed.

How High Is Too High?

In January 1988, the National Cholesterol Education Program (NCEP), a panel composed of national experts in blood cholesterol control, released an important report on the detection, evaluation, and treatment of high blood cholesterol in adults.

The report offers practical guidelines as well as specific recommendations for physicians and other health professionals on how to evaluate and treat persons with high blood cholesterol. The guidelines are part of a national campaign to educate physicians, health care professionals, and the general public about the importance of lowering blood cholesterol levels.

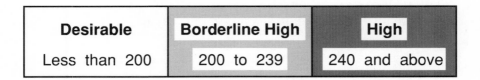

Desirable	Borderline High	High
Less than 200	200 to 239	240 and above

In the NCEP report, cholesterol levels in adults (20 years and older) are classified into three categories: levels below 200 mg/dl are classified as "desirable," those 200 to 239 mg/dl as "borderline high," and those 240 mg/dl and above as "high."

It is estimated that one out of every four adults, or about 40 million Americans, have "high" blood cholesterol, that is, 240 mg/dl and above. More than half of the adult population have blood cholesterol levels above 200 mg/dl, a level that is considered borderline.

Because the relationship between blood cholesterol levels and the risk of heart disease is a continuous and steadily increasing one (see chart 1, on page 4), these cutoff points are obviously somewhat arbitrary. The 240 mg/dl cutoff point for total blood cholesterol is a level at which the risk of heart disease is almost double that at 200 mg/dl and is rising sharply. Individuals with cholesterol levels at or above this point have sufficiently high risk to justify more detailed evaluation and possible treatment.

Assessing Your Risk

If your initial cholesterol number is elevated (above 200 mg/dl), you probably should have the test repeated to confirm the initial result. Getting more than one measurement before treatment is started is important, because cholesterol levels can vary, sometimes even considerably, from day to day. For the same reason, it is important that you do not change your eating habits during this series of baseline tests.

Along with cholesterol testing, and as part of your medical examination, your doctor will look for the presence of other risk factors. He or she will inquire about smoking and about prior history of heart disease affecting you or your family. Your doctor will also measure your blood pressure and check your weight.

Generally, if you have additional risk factors, your risk of heart disease is multiplied. For example, if your cholesterol level is high (240 mg/dl and above) and you have no other risk factors, your risk

Additional Risk Factors Checklist

You are considered to have a high-risk status for coronary heart disease if you have one of the following (in addition to high blood cholesterol):

Either:

☐ You already have coronary disease (a history of angina, heart attack, balloon angioplasty, or bypass surgery)

Or two of the following:

☐ You smoke cigarettes

☐ You have high blood pressure

☐ A parent, brother, or sister had a history of coronary heart disease before the age of 55

☐ You have diabetes

☐ You have a history of a stroke or blood vessel disease

☐ You are significantly overweight

☐ Your HDL-cholesterol level is too low (below 35 mg/dl)

☐ You are a male

is doubled. If, in addition to high cholesterol, you have high blood pressure, your risk increases fourfold. If you are also a smoker, your risk increases more than eightfold! As you can see, the presence of additional risk factors multiplies the chance of heart disease and may justify beginning treatment at a lower cholesterol level.

If your cholesterol level is "desirable" (under 200 mg/dl) at this initial test, you will be given general advice and educational materials on diet and other preventive measures, and you will be

Your Risk Category—And What to Do about It

Based on your cholesterol number and additional risk factors you may have (see checklist), select one of the following:

☐ *Your cholesterol level is "Desirable"*

Watch your diet to prevent your cholesterol from rising. Check your cholesterol within 5 years or at your next physical examination.

☐ *Your cholesterol level is "Borderline high"*

Your risk is somewhat increased. It's time to make some changes in your eating habits. Have your cholesterol checked again within a year.

☐ *Your cholesterol level is "Borderline high" **and** you have coronary heart disease or two other risk factors*

See the "high" category.

☐ *Your cholesterol level is "high"*

Your risk is increased. You should pay close attention to your cholesterol level and modify your eating habits and lifestyle, preferably under your doctor's supervision.

advised to have another cholesterol test within 5 years or with your next physical examination.

If your cholesterol level is "borderline high" (between 200 and 239 mg/dl), your risk is somewhat increased. You could benefit from lowering your cholesterol level by making some changes in your eating habits. Your doctor will advise you how best to change your diet and lifestyle, and will provide dietary instructions designed to lower your cholesterol level. He or she will probably want to see you about once a year for further evaluation.

If your cholesterol level is "borderline high" and you have coronary heart disease or two other risk factors (see checklist, on page 15), or if your cholesterol level is in the "high" category (240 mg/dl and above), your potential risk to develop heart disease is high enough to justify more "aggressive" evaluation and treatment. That means it's time to get serious about changing your eating habits and lifestyle, preferably under your doctor's supervision.

3 More about "Good" and "Bad" Cholesterol

Cholesterol circulating in the bloodstream is made up of cholesterol present in the various lipoprotein fractions, including the LDLs and HDLs. Since the real "villain" is the cholesterol carried by the LDLs (LDL-cholesterol), the total cholesterol level (that is, the cholesterol number) gives only an estimate of the risk.

To get a more complete and accurate picture, your doctor may ask for a "lipid profile" that includes not only the total cholesterol level, but also the LDL-cholesterol, HDL-cholesterol, and triglyceride levels. The lipid profile provides a more precise estimate of the risk on which to base treatment decisions.

LDL—the "Bad" Cholesterol

Low density lipoproteins (LDLs) are the major carriers of cholesterol in the blood. LDLs transport cholesterol from the liver, where cholesterol is manufactured, to the body, where it is processed. If there is too much LDL-cholesterol in the blood, there will be increased deposits of cholesterol in the walls of the arteries. Studies have shown that the higher the level of LDL-cholesterol, the greater the risk of coronary heart disease. What you want, therefore, is a low LDL-cholesterol level.

LDL-cholesterol levels are more precise than total cholesterol levels for predicting the risk of coronary heart disease, and are therefore preferred by doctors for making decisions about treatments to lower cholesterol.

Based on the NCEP guidelines (see page 13), LDL-cholesterol levels are classified into three categories, according to the predicted risk: levels below 130 mg/dl are classified as "desirable," those 130 to 159 mg/dl as "borderline-high risk," and levels of 160 mg/dl or greater as "high risk."

Because most of the cholesterol in the blood is carried by the LDLs, total cholesterol will rise as LDL-cholesterol rises and will fall as the LDL figure falls. Since testing for total cholesterol is more available, less expensive, and does not require fasting, it is often used instead of LDL-cholesterol to monitor cholesterol levels over a period of time and in response to treatment. A total cholesterol level of 240 mg/dl corresponds roughly to an LDL-cholesterol of 160 mg/dl, while a total cholesterol of 200 mg/dl corresponds roughly to an LDL-cholesterol of 130 mg/dl.

You can lower your LDL-cholesterol level, and thus reduce your risk of heart disease, by changing the kinds of foods you eat. Specifically, you can do that by cutting down on foods that contain saturated fats and cholesterol. Although you will be primarily lowering your LDL-cholesterol level, your total cholesterol level will decrease as well.

HDL—the "Good" Cholesterol

The function of HDLs (high density lipoproteins) is to remove cholesterol from the body cells and deliver it to the liver and other sites, where it can be processed and eliminated. By their action, HDLs appear to protect the arteries against atherosclerosis. Studies have shown that people with higher levels of HDL-cholesterol tend to have a lower risk of heart attacks. What you want, therefore, is a high HDL-cholesterol level.

The average level of HDL-cholesterol in the U.S. population is 50 mg/dl. Any HDL-cholesterol level lower than 35 mg/dl is considered too low. A level of 35 mg/dl increases the risk of coronary heart disease by about 50 percent, while still lower levels increase the risk even more.

There is no doubt that heredity plays an important role in determining what the level of HDL-cholesterol will be in a given individual. In addition, however, a number of undesirable factors tend to lower the HDL-cholesterol level. These factors include cigarette smoking, obesity, and lack of exercise. A low HDL-cholesterol level combined with other risk factors, such as high blood pressure, cigarette smoking, or a history of heart disease in the family, is an especially dangerous combination.

You can raise a low HDL-cholesterol level, but only within narrow limits. As a matter of fact, it is much more difficult to raise a low HDL-cholesterol than it is to reduce an elevated LDL-cholesterol. Although there have been no studies showing the benefit of raising low HDL-cholesterol levels, the connection between a reduced HDL level and the risk of heart disease justifies the attempt to raise the level, particularly when this can be done by appropriate changes in lifestyle.

If your HDL-cholesterol is too low (below 35 mg/dl), particularly if you have other risk factors for heart disease, you should discuss the matter with your doctor. You should then take vigorous steps to reduce or eliminate as many of these risk factors as possible. You should quit smoking, lower your blood pressure, exercise regularly, and lose weight if overweight. These steps will help raise your HDL-cholesterol level, although you may have a hard time reaching a "normal" level. In any case, these measures are likely to be good for your heart and for your general health.

Remember:

• LDL-cholesterol is the "bad" cholesterol. It causes a build-up of fatty plaques in the arteries and increases the risk of coronary heart disease. What you want is a low LDL-cholesterol.

• HDL-cholesterol is the "good" cholesterol. It protects the arteries against the formation of fatty plaques and reduces the risk of coronary heart disease. What you want is a high HDL-cholesterol.

Desirable Levels of Blood Lipids

Total cholesterol	below 200 mg/dl
LDL-cholesterol	below 130 mg/dl
HDL-cholesterol	above 35 mg/dl
Triglycerides	below 250 mg/dl

The Cholesterol/HDL Ratio

Some laboratories calculate the cholesterol/HDL ratio, which is simply the total cholesterol level divided by the HDL-cholesterol level. For example, if total cholesterol is 200 mg/dl, and HDL-cholesterol is 50 mg/dl, then the ratio is 4.

Researchers have found that this ratio can more effectively predict the risk of heart disease than the total cholesterol level alone. The average cholesterol/HDL ratio for adults is about 5, and it corresponds to the average risk. You want to be at no higher than the average risk, and preferably lower.

A ratio of 5 corresponds to a total cholesterol of 200 mg/dl and an HDL-cholesterol of 40 mg/dl. The higher the ratio over 5, the greater the risk—the lower the ratio under 5, the lower the risk. For example, if the cholesterol ratio is 6.5, the risk of heart disease is about twice the average. If, on the other hand, the ratio is 3.5, the risk is only half the average.

Some people have a normal total cholesterol level but an abnormally low HDL-cholesterol. For example, a person with a total cholesterol of 180 mg/dl (normal) and an HDL-cholesterol of 30 (too low)—this gives an abnormal cholesterol/HDL ratio of 6. In many such cases the low HDL is due to genetic causes, and very often it will not respond to measures that generally would raise the HDL. The risk in such individuals has not been well defined yet, but it appears that such HDL levels do not necessarily increase the risk as long as the total cholesterol remains in the lower range.

If your ratio is too high, you can lower it either by lowering your total cholesterol, by increasing your HDL-cholesterol, or preferably by doing both. As we've already seen, you can lower your total cholesterol by eating foods that contain less saturated fat and cholesterol, and you can raise your HDL-cholesterol by giving up smoking, by exercising regularly, and by losing weight.

Sample Lab Report

Name: *John Smith*
Age: *56*
Date: *Oct. 20, 1989*

Total Cholesterol	*225*
HDL-cholesterol	*42*
LDL-cholesterol	*145*
Cholesterol/HDL ratio	*5.4*
Triglycerides	*190*

What about Triglycerides?

Triglycerides are manufactured in the liver (from fats, sugars, and alcohol) and then transported into the bloodstream. In the blood, they are carried, together with cholesterol, by the various lipoproteins. The main carrier of triglycerides is a specific type of lipoprotein, called very low density lipoproteins (VLDLs). After a meal, especially after a fatty meal, the number of VLDLs in the blood rises significantly. The triglycerides are transported to the various body tissues where they will be either stored in fat cells for future use, or broken down to produce energy.

> ### Remember:
>
> • The "lipid profile" provides a more precise estimate of your risk than a cholesterol test and is useful in making treatment decisions. It includes the total cholesterol, LDL, HDL, and triglyceride levels.
>
> • You can have your total cholesterol measured at any time of the day, whether or not you have just eaten. If you are scheduled for a lipid profile, however, you should be fasting for at least 12 hours before the test.
>
> • You can lower your LDL-cholesterol level by changing your eating habits, especially cutting down on saturated fats and cholesterol. If your HDL-cholesterol is too low, you can raise it by giving up smoking, exercising regularly, and losing weight.

Several studies have shown an apparent association between the blood levels of triglycerides and the increased risk of coronary heart disease. After careful analysis, however, it seems that the increased risk was probably due to the presence of other independent risk factors (such as high blood pressure, cigarette smoking, and obesity) which are often seen in such patients. In any event, that association is definitely not as strong as the one between the level of cholesterol and the risk of heart disease.

Triglycerides should be measured only after a 12-hour fast, because a meal can raise the triglyceride levels to a significant degree. Average values of triglycerides are around 150 mg/dl for men and 120 mg/dl for women. Triglycerides are considered a risk factor for heart disease (though a minor one) only at levels above 250 mg/dl.

Most cases of mild elevation of triglyceride levels seen by doctors are due to a variety of factors, the most common being obesity and eating too much fat and sugar. Other factors include excessive intake of alcohol, diabetes, and certain medications. Elevated triglyceride levels are also seen in patients with various genetic disorders of fat metabolism.

If your triglyceride level is too high, you can lower it by making changes in your lifestyle—losing weight if overweight, exercising regularly, restricting alcohol intake, and eating less fat and sugar. If your triglyceride level remains high despite these measures, or if it is above 250 mg/dl, you may want to consult with your doctor. He or she will look for medical causes for high triglycerides and may prescribe a specific treatment.

4 Eating Right: The Key to a Lower Cholesterol

In the previous chapters you've learned about the cholesterol test and what the various numbers mean. If your cholesterol level is too high, it should be encouraging for you to learn that most people can lower their cholesterol by simply changing the foods they eat. In fact, it usually takes only three to four weeks to see a change in blood cholesterol levels.

The cholesterol level is influenced by the amount and kinds of fats we consume. Diets rich in saturated fats and cholesterol tend to raise the cholesterol level, whereas diets rich in unsaturated fats help to keep it low. As we'll see in the following chapters, you can lower your cholesterol by following several simple guidelines:

- Reducing fat intake, especially saturated fats
- Reducing intake of dietary cholesterol
- Increasing intake of complex carbohydrates and fiber
- Achieving and maintaining a desirable body weight

The ABCs of Eating Right

Food is more than just a matter of taste—it's the stuff we're made of, the energy we run on. The food you eat affects every cell in your body, and it may even affect the way you feel each day. Therefore, it is important to gain an understanding of what constitutes the body's best raw materials and best fuel. It makes good sense to acquire some nutritional know-how.

The Nutrients

Nutrients are substances obtained from food and used in the body to promote growth, maintenance, and repair. Food contains six major nutrients: carbohydrates, fat, proteins, small amounts of vitamins and minerals, and water.

Carbohydrates are our main source of energy. They are easily digested and converted into glucose ("blood sugar"), which is the form of sugar found in the blood. Glucose provides energy for the brain, nervous system, and muscles. A limited amount of glucose is stored in the muscles and liver as a reserve fuel (glycogen), but any excess of glucose is stored as fat. We consume carbohydrates in foods like bread, whole grains, fruits, and vegetables.

Fat is our most concentrated form of energy, providing a reserve of energy in periods of low caloric intake. Fat also insulates the body, protects the skin and other tissues from dryness, and assists the body in its absorption of fat-soluble vitamins. Fat is found in foods of animal sources, such as meat, milk, butter, and dairy products. It can also be found in foods of plant origin, such as olives, peanuts, coconuts, and vegetable oils.

Proteins are used to build, repair, and maintain the cells of virtually every body tissue. They supply energy when the body's carbohydrate and fat reserves have been exhausted. We get proteins from eating foods such as meat, fish, eggs, and milk. Plant foods like beans, rice, wheat, seeds, and nuts contain proteins too.

Vitamins are substances needed by the body in very small amounts. They provide no energy or calories. They participate in the biochemical reactions inside us, and help process other nutrients (carbohydrates and fats) into energy. Likewise, they help to convert proteins into the building blocks of the cells.

Minerals are also needed in relatively small amounts and do not supply energy. We have minerals in our body tissues and fluids—in our blood, bones, teeth, and skin, for example. Minerals work along with vitamins to assist in food metabolism. They also participate in transmitting nerve messages, contracting and releasing the muscles, and regulating the body's fluid balance.

Water, sometimes called the "forgotten nutrient," is second only to oxygen as a prerequisite for life. Water is present in every cell and

Dietary Guidelines for Americans

- Eat a variety of foods
- Maintain desirable weight
- Avoid too much fat, saturated fat, and cholesterol
- Eat foods with adequate starch and fiber
- Avoid too much sugar
- Avoid too much sodium
- If you drink alcohol, do so in moderation

U.S. Department of Agriculture

constitutes two-thirds of our body weight. Water flushes away wastes, cools us through perspiration, keeps the skin and mucous membranes moist, and accomplishes other important functions as well. Fresh fruits and vegetables are excellent sources of water. In addition to eating plenty of these foods, we need to drink water too—as many as five to six glasses a day.

The energy content of a food depends on how much carbohydrate, fat, and protein it contains. The units for measuring the energy value of foods are *calories*. Carbohydrate and protein provide 4 calories per gram, while fat provides 9 calories per gram. The gram is a unit of weight in the metric system—there are approximately 28 grams in one ounce.

The Balanced Diet

• Variety in your diet is necessary if you want to obtain the proper balance of needed nutrients (proteins, carbohydrates, fats, vitamins, and minerals). Besides, a varied diet is more interesting and satisfying than a diet that contains a limited number of foods. Also, there are dozens of tasty new ways to combine familiar ingredients that you may never have thought of before.

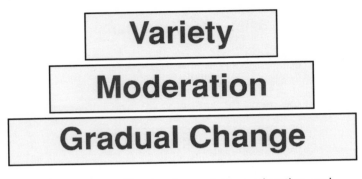

Remember: Emphasize variety, moderation and gradual change in your new approach to eating.

• Start thinking about how to make sensible selections within the framework of the basic food groups. In each food category, choose those foods that are lower in fat (especially saturated fats), lower in cholesterol, lower in added sugars, and lower in salt.

a) *Bread, cereals, pasta, legumes, and grains:* These foods are rich in complex carbohydrates, vitamins, and fiber. They are low in fat and contain no cholesterol. Combinations of dry legumes (dry beans and peas) with grains (corn, rice, wheat, and barley) can be used as substitutes for animal protein.

b) *Fruits and vegetables:* They are rich in natural sugars, complex carbohydrates, fiber, minerals, and vitamins. They are low in fat, calories, and sodium. They contain no cholesterol. The most nutritious way to eat fruits and vegetables is raw.

c) *Milk and dairy products:* These foods are good sources of protein, vitamins, and minerals (especially calcium). They contain fat as well. Low-fat and skim (nonfat) milk and dairy products are preferable to whole-milk products.

d) *Meat, poultry, fish, and eggs:* These foods are rich in protein, vitamins, and minerals. Unfortunately, they are also rich in fat, cholesterol, and calories, and should only be consumed in moderation (3 to 6 oz. a day). Fish, poultry (without the skin), and lean red meat are the preferred sources in this group.

e) *Vegetable fats and oils:* Should be used in small amounts.

• Moderation in your eating habits is important. Unless you have a specific health problem that requires you to avoid certain foods, there is no reason why you should completely give up foods you especially enjoy. It's often a question of tradeoffs. If you eat a high-fat food for one meal, choose those low in fat for the rest of your meals that day.

• Changes in the diet should be gradual. If changes are too abrupt, you are likely to resent them and will probably build up cravings for favorite foods you have excluded from your menu.

What You Can Expect

By closely following your diet and monitoring your progress with regular checkups, you can lower your cholesterol level and reduce your risk of heart disease. Generally, your cholesterol level will begin to drop about 3 to 4 weeks after you've started your new diet. Over time, you may reduce your total cholesterol level by 30 to 60 "points" (mg/dl), or even more.

How much you reduce your cholesterol level depends on how much fat, especially saturated fat, and how much cholesterol you were eating before starting your diet; how well you follow your new diet; and how responsive your body is to the diet. Generally, the higher your blood cholesterol level was to begin with, the greater the reduction you can expect with your new diet.

Your doctor will probably want to measure your cholesterol level after you've been on the diet for 4-6 weeks and again at 3 months. If your response to the diet has been satisfactory and your cholesterol goal has been met, you will enter a phase of long-term monitoring. This phase will involve remeasuring your cholesterol levels periodically.

If you haven't met your blood cholesterol goal in 3 months, your doctor may further restrict the saturated fat and cholesterol in your diet and enlist the help of a dietitian. Then, after 4-6 weeks more, and again after 3 months, he or she will measure your cholesterol level. If you have attained your goal, long-term monitoring can begin. If not, your doctor may decide you need medication along with your dietary changes.

Your new diet should be continued for life. While eating some foods high in saturated fats and cholesterol for one day or at one meal will not raise blood cholesterol levels, resuming old eating habits surely will. Surprisingly, after a while your new way of eating won't seem like a "diet" at all, but simply like your regular routine—full of appealing and appetizing foods.

You should also realize that changing eating patterns takes time. In fact, it may take you several weeks or months to incorporate all the changes you'll want to make in your diet. But the reward is worth it. Most likely you'll be shopping for some different foods, preparing some foods differently, even modifying your choices at restaurants and parties.

5 Cutting Back on Dietary Fat and Cholesterol

As we've seen, the first and most important step in lowering high blood cholesterol—whether caused by heredity or diet—is to change the kind of foods we eat. Among those changes, cutting back on fat and cholesterol is the most effective one. In this chapter, you'll learn the difference between saturated and unsaturated fats, the sources of fat and cholesterol in the foods we eat, and the steps you can take to reduce their amount in your diet.

In order to achieve the desired reduction, it is neither necessary nor desirable to give up all foods that contain fat. You can, instead, accomplish the reduction by making adjustments, such as eating fewer foods with a high fat content and selecting foods with lower fat content to replace them.

Types of Fat in the Foods We Eat

Fat is a general name for a class of compounds which do not dissolve in water. Depending on their chemical structure, dietary fats are classified into two basic types: saturated and unsaturated. Unsaturated fats are further classified into polyunsaturated and monounsaturated. The foods we eat contain mixtures of these different types of fat in varying proportions. No food contains pure saturated, polyunsaturated, or monounsaturated fat.

Saturated fats are generally solid at room temperature. They are usually found in foods of animal origin and dairy products but can also be found in some vegetable oils, such as coconut oil and palm oil. Unsaturated fats, on the other hand, are usually liquid at room temperature. They are predominantly of plant origin, and are found in vegetable oils, such as corn and safflower oils.

Most vegetable oils containing unsaturated fats can be converted from their natural liquid form to a form that is more solid and hardened. During the process, called hydrogenation, these oils become largely saturated, and thus resemble saturated fats in their appearance and the way the body processes them. A certain amount of hydrogenation is needed, for example, to produce margarines which spread easily at room temperature.

The cholesterol we consume is found exclusively in animal products. No cholesterol is found in foods of plant origin. Foods particularly high in cholesterol include egg yolks and organ meats, such as liver and brain.

Reducing Fat and Cholesterol in the Diet

The level of cholesterol in the blood is influenced by the amount and kinds of fats we eat. Diets using much saturated fats and cholesterol tend to raise the cholesterol level, whereas diets rich in unsaturated fats help to keep it low. You can lower your cholesterol by making certain changes in the foods you eat—reducing fat intake, especially saturated fats; using unsaturated fats instead of saturated ones; and decreasing dietary cholesterol.

Reducing Fat Intake, Especially Saturated Fats

Saturated fats raise your blood cholesterol level more than anything else in the diet. The best way to reduce your cholesterol level is to reduce the amount of saturated fats you eat.

Foods containing a large amount of saturated fats include: fatty cuts of meat, sausage, whole milk, cream, butter, ice cream, cheese, hydrogenated margarines, and bakery goods. These foods should be decreased, or consumed only occasionally. Foods with a lower fat content, and therefore preferable, include: lean cuts of red meat, chicken (without skin), fish, low-fat milk, skim (nonfat) milk, and low-fat dairy products.

Cholesterol-Lowering Diet Guidelines

Total fat	Less than 30% of total calories
Saturated fat	Less than 10% of total calories
Cholesterol	Less than 300 milligrams a day
Calories	To achieve and maintain desirable weight

A few vegetable fats—coconut oil, palm oil, and hydrogenated vegetable oil—are high in saturated fats. These vegetable fats are used in many commercially baked goods (such as cakes, cookies, and crackers), nondairy substitutes (coffee creamers, and whipped toppings), and snack foods (chips, candy bars, and popcorn). It is important that you read the label carefully when you purchase such products. (For more on food labels, see Chapter 7).

The typical American diet contains about 40 percent of total calories as fat, and 15 percent of total calories as saturated fat. As a first step toward lowering your cholesterol, it is recommended that you reduce your intake of total fat to less than 30 percent of total calories, and saturated fats to less than 10 percent of total calories. In Chapter 7, you'll learn how to determine your daily fat allowance, that is, the amount of fat you are "allowed" each day.

Using Unsaturated Fats Instead of Saturated Fats

Unsaturated fats actually help to lower cholesterol levels when substituted for saturated fats. Therefore, when you use fats, try using unsaturated (either poly- or monounsaturated) fats instead of saturated ones, whenever possible.

Polyunsaturated fats are found primarily in safflower, sunflower, corn, sesame, and soybean oils, which are common cooking oils. They are also commonly found in soft margarines, soft shortenings, and salad dressings.

Margarines vary considerably in their degree of saturation (or hydrogenation). In general, the more saturated a margarine is, the more solid it is at room temperature. Read the label carefully. The word "hydrogenated" or "hardened" on a label means that some of the unsaturated fat has been converted to saturated fat.

The most common source of monounsaturated fats is olive oil. Other sources are canola and peanut oils. Like other vegetable oils, these oils are used in cooking as well as in salads. Research has shown that substituting monounsaturated fats (or polyunsaturated fats) for saturated ones can reduce cholesterol levels.

Although unsaturated fats may help lower your cholesterol, it is not suggested that you consume them in large quantities. They are surely preferable to saturated fats, but there are good reasons to cut back on all fats. First, excessive fat intake of any kind contributes to weight gain. In addition, the effects of long-term consumption of large quantities of unsaturated fats are not known. In practical terms, you should reduce saturated fat intake considerably, and use small amounts of the more unsaturated fats instead.

Decreasing Dietary Cholesterol

Dietary cholesterol raises blood cholesterol levels, although not to the same degree as saturated fats do. Foods particularly rich in cholesterol are egg yolks and organ meats (liver, brain, and kidney). Other foods that contain cholesterol are dairy products, meat, poultry, fish, and shellfish. Foods of plant origin, like fruits, vegetables, grains, and cereals contain no cholesterol.

Since cholesterol is not really a fat (but rather a fat-like substance), it can be found in both high-fat and low-fat animal foods. In other words, even if a food is low in fat, it may be high in cholesterol. For instance, organ meats, like liver, are low in fat but very high in cholesterol.

The cholesterol content of meat is associated primarily with the lean tissue, not the fat. Equal weights of fatty and lean cuts of meat contain about equal amounts of cholesterol. Trimming meat is recommended not because it lowers the cholesterol content but because it reduces the saturated fat and caloric content.

Remember:

• Saturated fats raise your cholesterol level more than anything else in the diet. The best way to lower your blood cholesterol is to reduce the amount of saturated fats in the foods you eat.

• Unsaturated fats actually help to lower cholesterol levels when substituted for saturated fats. Therefore, when you use fats, choose unsaturated fats instead of saturated ones whenever possible.

• Dietary cholesterol raises blood cholesterol level, but not to the same degree as saturated fats do.

• The cholesterol we eat is found only in animal products. There is no cholesterol in foods of plant origin.

• A few vegetable fats (coconut oil, palm oil, and hydrogenated vegetable oil) are high in saturated fats.

The typical American diet supplies more than 500 milligrams of cholesterol a day over and above the amount of cholesterol made by the liver. The body's own cholesterol production decreases when cholesterol is eaten, but not enough to compensate for the amount consumed; therefore, blood cholesterol levels rise.

So, in addition to cutting back on total fat and saturated fat, it is recommended that you also reduce your cholesterol intake to less than 300 milligrams daily.

What about Fish Oils?

Until a few years back it was widely believed that consumption of fatty fish (such as salmon, mackerel, tuna, and herring) and shellfish should be avoided. Recent studies have shown, however,

Eating Well the Low-Fat Way

At the Supermarket

• When you buy red meat, choose lean cuts. Check for marbling (the white visible fat that runs through the meat), and avoid well-marbled cuts.

• Margarines vary considerably in their degree of saturation. As a general rule, the firmer the margarine, the more saturated it is. Soft tub margarines are preferred, because they are generally less saturated than stick margarines.

• Be aware that when you see "contains no cholesterol" on a label, you may still be getting a lot of fat in the product in the form of unsaturated or saturated vegetable fats.

In the Kitchen

• Trim off all visible fat before cooking your meat. Remove the skin from chicken and turkey.

• Choose cooking methods that use little or no fat. These include steaming, baking, broiling, grilling, and stir-frying in small amounts of fat. These methods are preferable to deep frying or stewing meats.

• Prepare pot roasts, soups, and stews a day in advance and chill them after cooking. The next day, skim off the congealed fat that has formed on top, then reheat.

• When sautéing or frying foods that don't need a lot of oil, brush the pan with oil just to coat it. Use a nonstick spray made from vegetable oil, or a nonstick pan that requires no greasing.

• When you cook, bake, or season your food, do not use saturated animal fats, such as butter or lard. Avoid solid (saturated) vegetable shortenings. Instead, use unsaturated vegetable oils and margarine.

that the kind of fats found in fatty fish and shellfish—unlike those found in red meat and poultry—are highly unsaturated.

These marine fats, termed omega-3 fatty acids, have been found to be useful in lowering blood cholesterol levels, as well as making the platelets (the tiny blood cells involved in clotting) less sticky. It has been suggested that by their actions, fish oils could actually prevent the build-up of fatty plaques and formation of blood clots inside the arteries. At this time, however, research is still at an early stage, and little is known about the actual benefits of fish oils in preventing coronary heart disease and strokes.

Press coverage has helped promote the use of fish-oil supplements. Capsules containing a variety of marine fatty acids are now available in pharmacies and health-food stores. However, the usefulness and safety of these supplements have not been established, and their use remains experimental. For these reasons, you should probably avoid the consumption of fish-oil supplements, at least until further clinical trials become available.

In the meantime, it is suggested that you consume marine oils by simply eating more fish. Besides, eating seafood is surely more enjoyable than swallowing fish-oil capsules. And there is ample room for fish as part of a well-balanced diet.

⑥ Where's the Fat? Making Better Food Choices

Following a low-fat, low-cholesterol diet is like a balancing act—getting the variety of foods necessary to supply the nutrients you need, yet keeping the amount of saturated fat, cholesterol, and calories to a minimum. A simple way to achieve this goal is to choose foods from the different food groups. This chapter will provide you with some basic information about the fat content of common foods, information that will assist you in making the right food choices for a low-fat, low-cholesterol diet.

To assure variety, and with it a balanced diet, every day try selecting foods from each of the groups below. Select different foods from within groups too, especially foods low in saturated fat. The number of portions and their size should be adjusted to reach and maintain your desirable weight.

Meat, Poultry, Fish, and Shellfish

Meat, poultry, fish, and shellfish are important sources of protein, vitamins, and minerals. However, they are also rich in saturated fats, cholesterol, and calories. Therefore, they should be consumed in moderation. Limit meat and fish consumption to one or two servings, no more than 6 ounces per day.

All animal protein sources—red meat, poultry, and fish—contain approximately equal amounts of cholesterol. So, when choosing meats, base your decision on the amount of saturated fat, not cholesterol, in those meats. Fish and poultry contain less total fat and less saturated fat than red meat, and are therefore the preferred sources of animal protein.

Red meat (beef, lamb, pork, veal) is a good source of animal protein and iron. The fat of red meats is mostly saturated. You can reduce the amount of fat by choosing lean cuts and trimming all fat off the outside of meat before cooking. The problem with red meat, however, is that much of the fat is marbled throughout the meat and will remain there even after cooking.

Red meat is graded as "prime," "choice," or "good." "Prime," the top grade, is more tender, more flavorful, and more expensive. It is usually fattier as well, since the grade is largely determined by how well marbled the meat is (marbling is the white streaks of fat in the meat). Less well-marbled cuts of meat can be almost as tender and tasty if prepared appropriately, and they are lower in saturated fat. Therefore, whenever possible, choose "choice" and "good" grades instead of "prime."

Although relatively rich in saturated fats, red meat need not be totally eliminated from your diet. Lean meat is rich in protein and is an important source of iron. Women before menopause, in particular, should not reduce consumption of red meat since this may increase the risk of iron-deficiency anemia.

Chicken and turkey are good sources of protein and an excellent choice for your diet. They can be substituted for lean red meat, but they do not contain as much iron. Remove the skin and underlying fat layers to reduce saturated fat content. Limit goose, duck, and most processed poultry products like bologna and hot dogs, which are very high in saturated fat. And, of course, chicken and turkey should not be fried in fats or covered with fat-rich sauces.

Chicken breast (light meat) without the skin is the part of the bird lowest in fat and thus your best choice. The leanest poultry meat is turkey breast. Dark meat, such as the leg portion, contains two to three times as much saturated fat as light meat, but is still lower in saturated fats then even the leanest red meats.

Fish is also a good source of animal protein. Fish contains cholesterol, but is usually lower in saturated fat than red meat and poultry. As we've seen, fish also is a good source of omega-3 fatty acids, a unique component of fish oils that appears to lower blood cholesterol. Eating fish about three times a week is a good and tasty way to help you cut back on saturated fat. *Shellfish* (such as shrimp, lobster, and crab) are relatively high in cholesterol but are low in fat, and thus may be eaten in moderation.

Be careful not to undermine the excellent properties of seafood by adding saturated fat to your dishes when cooking or serving them. Broiling, baking, and poaching are preferable to deep frying. If you pan-fry or sauté your fish, use a small amount of unsaturated oil, or try a cooking spray or a nonstick pan. When you serve seafood, use a twist of lemon instead of butter or fat-rich sauces.

Processed meats (such as bacon, bologna, salami, sausage, and hot dogs) should be eaten infrequently. They contain large quantities of fat, and 60 to 80 percent of their calories come from fat, much of it saturated. *Organ meats* (liver, brain, kidney, and sweetbread) are relatively low in fat; however they are very rich in cholesterol, and they should also be limited.

Milk and Dairy Products

Milk and dairy products are good sources of protein, vitamins, and calcium. However, they contain fat and cholesterol as well. In fact, ounce for ounce, most cheeses have more saturated fat than lean cuts of red meat and poultry, and about the same amount of cholesterol.

Milk is characterized by its fat content. Whole milk is about 3.3 percent fat—this means that 3.3 percent of the total weight is contributed by fat. This amount may seem trivial, hardly worth counting. However, most of the weight of milk is accounted for by water. In terms of calories, fat accounts for half of the total calories, thus making whole milk a high-fat food. Most of the fat in milk products is saturated regardless of whether it is whole, low-fat 2%, or low-fat 1% milk. This is true of all dairy products, including cheese, yogurt, cream, and ice cream.

Both low-fat 1% and skim (nonfat) milk provide the same nutrients as whole milk (3.3%) or low-fat 2% milk, while providing much less saturated fat and cholesterol and fewer calories. Try easing your way from whole milk to low-fat 2% milk, then to low-fat 1% milk, and finally to skim milk. Make the change gradually, over a period of several weeks.

Milk is an important source of calcium. Calcium is vital for developing and maintaining strong bones. To help maintain your calcium intake, try having at least 2 servings per day of low-fat or nonfat dairy products, such as low-fat 1% milk, skim milk, low-fat cottage cheese, and low-fat or nonfat yogurt.

Most *cheeses*, while high in calcium, are also high in saturated fat and cholesterol. Natural and processed hard cheeses, which are made of whole milk, have the highest fat content. In fact, whole-milk cheeses derive over 80 percent of their calories from fat, and over half of those calories are contributed by saturated fat.

Imitation cheeses made with vegetable oils, part-skim milk cheeses, and cheeses advertised as "low-fat" are usually lower in saturated fat and cholesterol than are natural and processed cheeses. However, even part-skim milk cheeses and "low-fat" cheeses are not necessarily lower in fat than many meats. Whenever possible, substitute low-fat and imitation cheeses for natural, processed, and hard cheeses. Read the label and choose low-fat cheeses that have between 2 and 5 grams of fat per ounce.

Ice cream is made from whole milk and cream and therefore contains a considerable amount of saturated fat and cholesterol. You don't have to eliminate ice cream, but try eating it in small amounts and less often. Instead of ice cream, you might try other *frozen desserts* such as ice milk, low-fat or nonfat yogurt, and sherbet—all of which are low in saturated fats.

Eggs

Egg yolks are very rich in cholesterol. A single large egg contains about 250 mg of cholesterol (nearly your entire day's quota of cholesterol), concentrated totally in the yolk. Egg yolks often are hidden in cooked and processed foods. Egg whites contain no cholesterol, and are an excellent low-calorie source of protein; they can be eaten often.

Eat no more than three egg yolks a week including those in processed foods and baked goods. Experiment with 1-2 whites instead of whole eggs in recipes, or use commercial egg substitutes that do not contain egg yolk.

Healthy Ways to Prepare and Serve Foods

Even the most nutritious foods may lose their nutritional value when they are prepared or served the wrong way. Cooking healthfully is an easy way to reduce or control the fat in your diet. All it takes is a little practice. And once you've tried it for a while, you'll appreciate the fresh, less greasy taste of your food.

Instead of:	Try:
Frying, deep-frying	Baking, broiling, steaming
Butter, lard, shortening	Margarine
Shortening for greasing pans	Nonstick cooking spray
A whole egg	Two egg whites
Whole milk, cream	Skim or low-fat milk
Sour cream	Low-fat yogurt
Cream cheese	Farmer cheese
Mayonnaise spread	Mustard
Creamy salad dressings	Oil and vinegar
Commercial baked goods, prepared mixes	Homemade baked goods using unsaturated fats
Vegetables prepared in butter or cream sauces	Fresh, frozen, or canned vegetables
Added fat, butter, margarine, cream sauce, gravy	Wine, herbs and spices, lemon juice, broth for cooking and sautéeing

Egg substitutes consist almost entirely of egg whites, and thus contain little or no cholesterol. Some have added nonfat dry milk, and some contain a small amount of fat. Egg substitutes are available in powder and liquid forms, and are generally found in the frozen product section of your supermarket.

Fats and Oils

As we've seen, saturated fats in your diet raise blood cholesterol level while unsaturated fats tend to keep it low. Therefore, you should reduce the intake of fats and oils that are high in saturated fats. Butter, lard, and beef fat are examples of cholesterol-raising animal fats, and they should be reduced as much as possible.

Vegetable fats do not contain cholesterol (only animal products contain cholesterol). Beware, however. Certain vegetable fats, especially coconut oil and palm oil, are very high in cholesterol-raising saturated fats and should be avoided. These fats are often used in bakery goods, processed foods, popcorn oils, and nondairy creamers. Read the label very carefully to detect the presence of these saturated vegetable oils.

Unsaturated vegetable fats and oils do not raise cholesterol, but they should be limited because they are high in calories. Generally, up to 6 to 8 teaspoons a day is acceptable. Desirable liquid vegetable oils are corn, olive, peanut, canola, safflower, soybean, and sunflower oils. Peanut butter may be eaten in small amounts.

Margarine is made of partially hydrogenated vegetable oil and is preferable to butter. Margarines vary considerably in their degree of saturation. As a general rule, the firmer the margarine the more saturated it is. Soft tub margarines are preferred, because they are generally less saturated than stick margarines. Vegetable shortenings fall into the same category as margarine.

Mayonnaise and *salad dressings* generally are made from unsaturated fats, but they too should be limited because of their high caloric content.

Peanuts, nuts, and seeds tend to be high in fat, but the fat usually is unsaturated. You should limit their intake mainly to avoid excess calories. The same is true for peanut butter.

Breads, Cereals, Pasta, Rice, and Dried Beans and Peas

These products are high in complex carbohydrates and low in fat. Therefore, they can be increased in the diet as substitutes for fatty foods. However, they too contain calories, and must not be eaten in excess. Dried legumes (beans and peas) are good sources of protein, and they can be used instead of meat.

Try pasta, rice, and legumes as main dishes, in casseroles, soups, or other one-dish meals, without high-fat sauces. Also, try pasta, rice, legumes, and vegetables with smaller amounts of lean meat, poultry, fish, or shellfish to derive complete protein sources with less fat and calories.

Cereal products are usually low in saturated fat. Exceptions to this include the many types of granolas and other cereals that contain coconut or coconut oil. Breads and most rolls are also low in fat. However, many types of commercially baked goods (such as croissants, muffins, biscuits, butter rolls, and doughnuts) are made with large amounts of saturated fats. Be sure and read the labels on these products to determine their fat content.

Fruits and Vegetables

Fruits and vegetables contain no cholesterol and are very low in fat and low in calories. The exceptions are avocados and olives, which are high in fat (mostly unsaturated) and calories.

Fruits and vegetables should be an essential part of every meal. By eating fruits as snacks and desserts, and vegetables as snacks and side dishes, you'll be increasing your intake of vitamins, minerals, and fiber while at the same time lowering your intake of saturated fat and cholesterol.

Sweets and Snacks

Sweets and snacks (such as cakes, pies, cookies, cheese crackers, and chips) often are high in saturated fat, cholesterol, and calories. Some of these products, however, may contain unsaturated fats or may be low in total fat and calories. Once again, the key is to read the label carefully.

If you are accustomed to eating commercially prepared pies, cakes, or cookies—all of which are high in saturated fat—there are some very tasty alternatives available. A few examples of acceptable commercially prepared desserts include angel food cake, fig bars, and ginger snaps. As an alternative, try fruit for dessert. And for your next snack, try a piece of fruit, some vegetables, or a low-fat snack like unbuttered popcorn or breadsticks.

	Choose	**Decrease**
Meat, Poultry, Fish, and Shellfish (up to 6 ounces a day)	Lean cuts of meat (beef, lamb, pork, veal) Poultry (chicken, turkey) without skin Fish Shellfish	Fatty cuts of meat (corned beef brisket, regular ground beef, short ribs, spareribs) Organ meats Luncheon meats Sausage, hot dogs, bacon
Milk and Dairy Products (2 to 3 servings a day)	Skim or low-fat 1% milk Buttermilk Nonfat or low-fat yogurt Low-fat soft cheeses (such as cottage cheese) Cheeses with less than 5 grams of fat an ounce **Go easy on:** Low-fat 2% milk Regular yogurt Part-skim ricotta cheese Part-skim or imitation hard cheeses "Light" cream cheese "Light" sour cream	Whole milk Cream, half and half, most nondairy creamers, imitation milk products, whipped cream Whole-milk cottage cheese, whole-milk ricotta cheese Hard cheeses (such as Swiss, American, mozzarella, cheddar, Muenster) Cream cheese Sour cream
Eggs (no more than 3 egg yolks a week)	Egg whites Cholesterol-free egg substitutes	Egg yolks
Fats and Oils (up to 6 to 8 teaspoons a day)	Unsaturated vegetable oils (corn, olive, peanut, canola, safflower, soybean, sunflower) Margarine or shortening from unsaturated oils Salad dressings from unsaturated oils **Go easy on:** Nuts and seeds Avocados and olives	Butter, lard, bacon fat, coconut oil, palm oil Shortening made from saturated fats listed above Dressings made with egg yolk

Chart 2

	Choose	**Decrease**
Breads, Cereals, Pasta, Rice, Dried Beans and Peas (6 or more servings a day)	Breads (such as white, whole wheat, rye) Bagel, English muffin, sandwich buns, rolls Low-fat crackers (bread sticks, rye krisp, saltines) Cooked cereals, most ready-to-eat cereals Pasta (noodles, spaghetti) Rice (white or brown) Dried beans and peas, soybeans, tofu **Go easy on:** Store-bought pancakes, waffles, biscuits, muffins	Commercial baked goods (croissants, butter rolls, sweet rolls, danish pastry, doughnuts) Most snack crackers (such as cheese crackers, butter crackers, those made with saturated oils) Granola-type cereals made with saturated oils Pasta and rice prepared with cream, butter, or cheese sauces Egg noodles
Fruits and Vegetables (2 to 4 servings of fruit, 3 to 5 servings of vegetables a day)	Fresh, frozen, or canned fruits and vegetables	Vegetables prepared in butter, cream, or sauce
Sweets and Snacks (avoid too many sweets)	Low-fat frozen desserts (sherbet, frozen yogurt) Low-fat cakes (such as angel food cake) Low-fat cookies (such as fig bars, gingersnaps) Low-fat candy (such as jelly beans, hard candy) Low-fat snacks (such as plain popcorn, pretzels) Nonfat beverages (juices, soda water, coffee) **Go easy on:** Frozen desserts (such as ice milk) Homemade cakes, pies, and cookies, using unsaturated oils	High-fat frozen desserts (such as ice cream, frozen tofu) Most store-bought cakes, pies, cookies Chocolate bars, other high-fat candy High-fat snacks (such as chips, buttered popcorn) High-fat beverages (milkshakes)

Helpful Tips

Dining Out the Healthy Way

• When reading the menu, choose foods described in terms suggestive of low-fat preparation, such as: steamed, in its own juice, garden fresh, broiled, roasted, poached, tomato juice, dry broiled (in lemon juice or wine).

• Avoid ordering foods described in any of the following terms: buttery, in butter sauce; sautéed, fried, crispy, braised; creamed, in cream sauce, in its own gravy, hollandaise; au gratin, Parmesan, in cheese sauce, escalloped; marinated (in oil), basted; casserole, prime, hash, and pot pie.

• For an appetizer, enjoy steamed seafood, raw vegetables, and fresh melon or other fruits. Avoid high-fat items such as patés, cream soups, quiches, and fried zucchini.

• For an entree, your best choices are chicken, seafood, and vegetable dishes. Lean red meats, when properly trimmed and prepared, are also acceptable. Look for simply prepared items. Avoid casseroles and foods with heavy sauces.

• Salad dressings are high in fat and calories. It is best to order dressings "on the side," so you can control the amount you use. Limit high-fat toppings such as bacon, crumbled eggs, cheese, sunflower seeds, and olives.

• Ask for margarine instead of butter, and limit the amount of margarine used on bread. On your baked potato, use yogurt or margarine instead of sour cream or butter.

• Side dishes of vegetables and starches are good complements to your meal, but choose those cooked with no fat (that is, boiled, baked, or steamed), rather than those fried or covered with sauce or cream.

• For dessert, choose fresh fruit, low-fat or nonfat yogurt, and fruit ices instead of pastries, cookies, and ice cream. Also acceptable are angel food cake, jello, and sherbet.

	Limit	**Choose**
Chinese	Fried noodles, egg-drop soup, deep-fried shrimp, egg rolls	Steamed or lightly sautéed fish, chicken, stir-fried vegetables, steamed rice
French	Butter, cream sauces, rich pastries and desserts	Broiled lean meats, vegetables, fruit, French bread, sorbet
Italian	Dishes with cream sauces, custard, heavily buttered garlic bread, cheesecake, ice cream, and pastries	Pasta, chicken or fish dishes, tomato-based (marinara) sauce, Italian bread, salad with oil and vinegar, ices, fresh fruit
Japanese	Deep-fried dishes (tempura), high-sodium soups and sauces	Sushi, sashimi, chicken teriyaki, steamed rice
Mexican	Fried tortilla chips, sour cream, refried beans, cheese sauces	Chicken enchiladas, chicken tostada, gazpacho, lean beef or chicken fajitas, rice, beans (not refried), salsa, flour tortillas
American	High-fat meats, sour cream, buttered biscuits, creamy salad dressings, gravy	Roasted turkey or broiled fish, baked potato, vegetables, fresh fruit
Fast food	Double burgers, bacon cheese burgers, milk shakes, pizza with meat toppings, French fries, hot dogs	Salad bar fruits and vegetables, roast beef sandwich, vegetable or skim-milk mozzarella pizza, baked potato (no cheese sauce)

Chart 3. Your Basic Guide to Ethnic Restaurants

7 How Much Fat? From Theory to Practice

As you've learned, the best way to lower your cholesterol is to cut back on dietary fat. More specifically, your diet should contain no more than 30 percent of its total calories from fat, with less than 10 percent from saturated fat. That's fine in theory, you may say, but what does it mean in practical terms? In this chapter, you'll learn how to translate these theoretical numbers into practical ones you can use when making food selections.

Your Daily Fat Allowance

Your daily fat allowance is the actual amount of fat (in grams) you are "allowed" to eat each day to meet your body's energy needs while staying within the above guidelines. You can determine your fat allowance in three easy steps. And once you've done that, you'll be able to use that number without recalculating it each time.

Step 1: Determine your desirable body weight

Your desirable (or ideal) weight is how much you should weigh (not how much you actually weigh), based on your height and body frame type. The taller and bigger your are, the higher the number of calories you need each day.

You can determine your desirable weight by referring to the weight and height chart on page 88, Chapter 10. Find your height in the left-hand column. Then move across the page to the body frame that best describes you.

For the purpose of the weight table, your body frame is "small" if you can wrap your left thumb and middle finger around your right wrist and have these two digits overlap. If the thumb and finger barely touch, then you have a "medium" body frame. If they don't touch at all, you have a "large" build. This method is a bit crude, but accurate enough for our purpose.

Step 2: Determine your daily caloric needs

You need a certain number of calories each day to meet your energy expenditures. This number is your daily caloric needs. It depends on several factors, including your desirable body weight (from step 1), your activity level, and your gender:

- *Your activity level.* The more active you are, the more calories you burn each day, and the more calories you'll need to consume. Choose one of the following three descriptions that most accurately describes your level of activity:

    - Sedentary: You spend much of your time in a sitting position and are not involved in any regular exercise activities.
    - Fairly active: You are involved in exercise (such as walking, jogging, swimming, tennis, etc.) on a regular basis, at least three times a week.
    - Very active: You perform vigorous exercise activities for extended periods of time, almost daily.

- *Your gender.* Men and women have different metabolisms. Men for the most part burn more calories per pound of body weight than women. An average adult male, for example, requires about 15 calories to maintain each pound of weight. An average female requires only about 13 calories per pound of weight.

To determine your daily caloric needs, use chart 4. First, locate your desirable weight along the left-hand column. Then, making sure you use the correct table for your gender, find your daily caloric needs number under the column corresponding to your activity level. If your activity level changes, as it might with changes in the seasons, you should re-determine that number.

Lbs.	Sedentary	Fairly Active	Very Active
Men			
120	1560	1800	2040
125	1625	1875	2125
130	1690	1950	2210
135	1755	2025	2295
140	1820	2100	2380
145	1885	2175	2465
150	1950	2250	2550
155	2015	2325	2635
160	2080	2400	2720
165	2145	2475	2805
170	2210	2550	2890
175	2275	2625	2975
180	2340	2700	3060
185	2405	2775	3145
190	2470	2850	3230
195	2535	2925	3315
200	2600	3000	3400
Women			
100	1100	1300	1500
105	1155	1365	1575
110	1210	1430	1650
115	1265	1495	1725
120	1320	1560	1800
125	1375	1625	1875
130	1430	1690	1950
135	1485	1755	2025
140	1540	1820	2100
145	1595	1885	2175
150	1650	1950	2250
155	1705	2015	2325
160	1760	2080	2400
165	1815	2145	2475
170	1870	2210	2550
175	1925	2275	2625
180	1980	2340	2700

Chart 4. Your daily caloric needs, based on your desirable weight, activity level, and gender (see text).

Step 3: Determine your daily fat allowance

Once you've found your daily caloric needs, you can easily determine your daily fat allowance—the amount of fat in grams you are allowed each day. Simply round off your daily caloric needs value to the nearest hundred, then locate this new value along the left-hand column in chart 5. You'll get two numbers: one for the total fat allowed daily (corresponding to 30 percent of total calories), the other for the saturated fat allowed daily (corresponding to 10 percent of total calories).

Example: A 160-pound man, who is at his desirable weight (not too heavy, not too lean) and fairly active (jogs three times a week and plays tennis on weekends), can maintain his current weight on 2,400 calories a day. To control his cholesterol he should limit his total fat intake to no more than 80 grams and his saturated fat intake to no more than 27 grams each day.

[If you prefer, you can calculate your daily fat allowance on your own. First, multiply your daily caloric needs value by 30 percent (or 0.3). The value you get is the number of calories from fat you are allowed each day to stay within the guidelines. Then, divide this number by 9 (since each gram of fat provides 9 calories). This is your total fat allowance. In the same way, you can calculate your daily saturated fat allowance, by first multiplying your daily caloric needs value by 10 percent (or 0.1), and then dividing it by 9.]

· · · · · ·

If you look at food labels, you will usually (but not always) see a complete breakdown of carbohydrate, protein, and fat. If nutrition information is not available on the package, use this book's food tables in the appendix to find the fat content and saturated fat content of various foods. The amount in a given serving is represented in grams. By becoming familiar with the amount of fat in various foods, you'll quickly start thinking about the amount of fat in grams you need each day.

No one is expected to memorize the breakdown of each and every food. But you can start picking up on trends. You'll notice, for example, that beef has more fat than chicken, and that chicken has more fat than fish. And you'll be the one to decide whether to choose the fat in beef or the fat in fish on any given day.

Cals.	Total fat allowed (in grams)	Saturated fat allowed (in grams)
1100	37	12
1200	40	13
1300	43	14
1400	47	16
1500	50	17
1600	53	18
1700	57	19
1800	60	20
1900	63	21
2000	67	22
2100	70	23
2200	73	24
2300	77	26
2400	80	27
2500	83	28
2600	87	29
2700	90	30
2800	93	31
2900	97	32
3000	100	33
3100	103	34
3200	107	36
3300	110	37
3400	113	38

Chart 5. Your daily fat allowance, based on your daily caloric needs (see text).

Your Daily Fat Allowance — Worksheet

Step 1: Determine your *desirable body weight,* based on your gender, height, and body frame (chart 6, page 88).

Your desirable body weight: _____ lbs.

Step 2: Determine your *daily caloric needs,* based on your desirable body weight, activity level, and gender (chart 4).

Your daily caloric needs: _____ cals.

Step 3: Determine your *daily fat allowance,* based on your daily caloric intake (chart 5).

Total fat allowed: _____ grams

Saturated fat allowed: _____ grams

What about Your Cholesterol Allowance?

As you know, it is the saturated fat in your diet that, for the most part, raises your blood cholesterol level. However, dietary cholesterol can raise blood cholesterol level as well. So, you should also cut down on the amount of cholesterol in your diet. To stay within the guidelines, you should limit your cholesterol intake to no more than 300 mg (this is milligrams, not grams) per day.

As we've already mentioned, the only source of cholesterol in the diet is from animal-derived foods and products. There is no cholesterol in foods of plant origin, such as grains, cereals, bread, fruits, and vegetables. Therefore, by cutting back on fat, especially saturated fats from animal sources, you'll automatically cut back on dietary cholesterol.

Reading the Label

U.S. government regulations require that all enriched or fortified foods, and foods for which a nutrition claim is made, include nutrition information on the label. This information is divided into three categories:

1) *Nutrition Information per Serving.* It includes: serving size; servings per container; calories per serving; and protein, carbohydrate, and fat in grams per serving.

2) *Percentage of the U.S. Recommended Daily Allowances (U.S. RDA).* The amounts of vitamins A, C, thiamine, riboflavin, and niacin are listed as a percentage of the U.S. RDA. Two minerals, calcium and iron, are also listed. Protein is shown as a percentage of the U.S. RDA, as well as in weight by grams.

3) *Ingredient Labeling.* Most packaged foods will also list ingredients on the label. Each ingredient must be listed in order of its concentration in the product with the ingredient in largest quantity first, down to the ingredient in smallest quantity last.

The number of calories per serving is listed on the label. Calories depend on the amount of fat, protein, and carbohydrate in the food. Fat, which has the most calories, supplies 9 calories per gram. Protein and carbohydrate supply 4 calories per gram. Calories are often rounded to the nearest 10.

Present labeling regulations allow only two kinds of fat to be listed, polyunsaturated and saturated. Although monounsaturated fat may make up a considerable part of the total fat in a food, it is not listed separately. Remember that all kinds of fat (whether saturated, monounsaturated, or polyunsaturated) have the same caloric value, 9 calories per gram.

Cholesterol content does not have to be listed on food labels, but it may be listed if the manufacturer so wishes. If cholesterol is listed, it must be shown in two ways—as "milligrams (mg) of cholesterol per serving" and as "milligrams per 100 grams of food."

Real Mayonnaise

Nutrition Information per Serving

Serving size	1 tablespoon (14 grams)
Servings per container	16
Calories per serving	100
Protein	0 grams
Carbohydrate	0 grams
Fat	11 grams
Polyunsaturated	5 grams
Saturated	2 grams
Cholesterol (50 mg/100 grams)	8 milligrams
Sodium	80 milligrams

Percentage of the U.S. Recommended Daily Allowances (U.S. RDA)

Contains less than 2 percent of the U.S. RDA of protein, vitamin A, vitamin C, thiamine, riboflavin, niacin, calcium, iron.

Ingredients

Soybean oil, whole eggs, vinegar, water, egg yolks, salt, sugar, and lemon juice

To assist you even further in getting the most nutritive value for your money, producers may also choose to identify nutrients in foods that don't require labeling. For example, fresh meats, poultry, fish, fruits and vegetables are sometimes labeled although it is not required. Producers may also list information about saturated and unsaturated fat, cholesterol, sodium, and additional vitamins.

When making a comparison between foods, be sure to do it on the basis of the serving size and the number of servings per container listed on the label as well as what *you* consider a serving size.

Making Sense of Claims

Food manufacturers have become very skilled at packaging their products so you're convinced the contents are good for you. They are required by law to be truthful, but keep in mind that their goal is to sell their product. Some of the bright, bold claims you read—although not untruthful—can be misleading. As a consumer, you should learn to interpret those claims.

Following is a list of claims that often appear on labels, along with some suggestions to help you determine their meanings.

"No cholesterol" or *"cholesterol free"*. It means just that. The food contains no cholesterol. Manufacturers often use these claims on foods, such as margarine and vegetable oils, to suggest that other margarines and vegetable oils do contain cholesterol. But as you already know, no margarine, vegetable oil, or shortening made from vegetable products contain cholesterol (whether they are white, yellow, liquid, or solid).

Also, just because a product is labeled *no cholesterol, cholesterol free*, or *vegetable oil*, don't assume it's necessarily good for you. Some vegetable fats, such as coconut and palm oils, contain no cholesterol but are highly saturated and therefore bad for you.

"90% fat free" or *"10% fat"*. This kind of statement is often found on packaged cold cuts (such as sliced ham and salami). It means that 10 percent of the product by *weight* is fat. But weight is not the crucial factor (since much of the weight is from water)—calories are. Products that are "90% fat free" usually contain over 50 percent of their calories from fat.

Though the manufacturer is correct in a technical sense, these products are not low-fat foods. To get around this problem, purchase products that give you the exact amount of fat in grams—that's a figure you can count on.

"Light" or *"lite"*. As surprising as it may sound, these terms have no specific meaning. It doesn't necessarily mean that the food has less fat or fewer calories. It may simply mean that the

product weighs less, has a lighter texture, or has a lighter color! Read the label carefully to see exactly what the fat content is.

"Non-dairy". All it means is that the food contains no fat from milk. But beware. Many of these products, especially nondairy creamers and whipped toppings, are rich in saturated fats, such as coconut oil or palm oil, that raise blood cholesterol. Once again, check the label for the type of fat in the product.

Using Food Tables

Food tables can be very helpful, especially if you are on a cholesterol-lowering diet. They provide you with information about the fat content of various foods, thereby allowing you to choose, based on your own preferences, combinations of foods that can fit into your daily fat budget. You can use this book's comprehensive food tables in the appendix to figure out the fat, saturated fat, and cholesterol content of various foods.

Keeping Track of Your Fat Intake

If you really want to cut back on dietary fat, you must first figure out how much fat you actually eat. The best way to keep track of your fat intake is to keep a food record. But don't worry—you won't have to do this for the rest of your life. After a few days of practice you'll get a pretty good idea of which foods allow you to stay within your fat budget.

Write down everything you eat for a period of three days (or more). Don't forget those "light" snacks (such as that handful of peanuts you grabbed before dinner). Record one food on each line and write down the portion size and how it was prepared (see Sample Food Record). Use the information from the label or from this book's food tables to determine the amount of calories, total fat, saturated fat, and cholesterol in each food. Then add up the numbers. You may be surprised at the results.

Sample Food Record

Date _____

	Actual	Goal	
Calories	_____	_____	(cal.)
Total fat	_____	_____	(grams)
Saturated fat	_____	_____	(grams)
Cholesterol	_____	_____	(mg)

Food / Portion size	cals.	total fat	sat. fat	chol.
Total				

To be able to assess portion sizes accurately, you may need, at least initially, to measure the actual amounts of the foods you eat. In addition to using measuring spoons and measuring cups, you may find an inexpensive kitchen scale helpful. Use these measuring tools to determine the size of the serving you actually eat and compare it to the size of the serving listed on the label or food tables.

⑧ Fats Are Out, Carbohydrates Are In

Carbohydrates—which are contained in foods like bread, whole grains, fruits, and vegetables—are our main source of energy. They are easily digested and converted into glucose ("blood sugar"), which is the form of sugar found in the blood. Glucose provides energy for the brain, the nervous system, and the muscles. A limited amount of glucose is stored in the muscles and liver as a reserve fuel (glycogen), but any excess of glucose is stored as fat.

Carbohydrates: Simple and Complex

Depending on their chemical composition, carbohydrates come in two forms—simple and complex. Simple carbohydrates are rapidly broken down into glucose and absorbed into the blood. They give us an immediate energy jolt followed by an equally sudden energy drop. Complex carbohydrates, on the other hand, break down into glucose more slowly, providing us with sustained energy over an extended period of time.

Simple carbohydrates, or "sugars," occur naturally along with vitamins, minerals, and fiber in fresh fruits and some vegetables. They can also be found in concentrated form, in foods like honey and refined table sugar. The sugar we should avoid is the concentrated kind, not the dilute sugars in fruits and vegetables. (For more on sugar, see page 73).

Complex carbohydrates, also known as "starches," are found in a variety of plant foods such as potatoes, rice, corn, dried beans and peas, pasta, cereals, wheat, flour, and bread. They are also found in fresh fruits and vegetables. In their natural, unprocessed form, foods rich in complex carbohydrates are good sources of vitamins, minerals, and fiber. In addition, they are low in fat and they contain no cholesterol. From now on, complex carbohydrates should become the central part of your diet.

Complex Carbohydrates Are Good for You

Contrary to what many people think, complex carbohydrates are not "fattening." Ounce per ounce, they have the same number of calories as protein and less than half the calories of fat. Complex carbohydrates make us feel as though we've "eaten something." They give us something to chew on and fill our stomach, thus preventing us from overeating. What can make carbohydrate foods fattening are the high-calorie sauces, creams, dressings, and fats frequently added to them. As with any other foods, if carbohydrates are consumed in excess they can contribute to weight gain.

Complex carbohydrates make good low-cost substitutes for animal protein. Dried beans and peas are the richest source of vegetable protein. Unlike those of animal sources, proteins of vegetable origin are considered "incomplete," because they lack certain amino acids (the building blocks of proteins) necessary for the body to manufacture "complete" proteins. Therefore, they should preferably be used in combinations with other foods, termed "complementary proteins." The protein value of dried beans and peas, for example, can be improved by eating them together with grains, such as corn, rice, wheat, and barley.

Natural carbohydrate foods, particularly whole grains, fresh fruits, and vegetables, are excellent sources of dietary fiber. Based on their ability to dissolve in water, dietary fibers are grouped into two categories: soluble and insoluble. Soluble fiber, which is found in oat bran, dry beans and peas, and some fruits and vegetables, can lower blood cholesterol levels. Insoluble fiber is found in whole wheat, cereals, whole-wheat breads, fruits and vegetables. Insoluble fiber acts as a natural laxative and promotes regularity, but it has very little or no effect on blood cholesterol levels. (For more on dietary fiber, see Chapter 9).

Your Guide to Good Carbohydrates

Not all complex carbohydrates have equal nutritional value. Some contain many of the things that are good for you (such as vitamins, minerals, and fiber). Others have much or all of nature's goodness refined out of them, leaving behind little or nothing more than calories. Still others are prepared with too much fat or are served with rich, creamy sauces.

The following section will enable you to select and prepare foods that give you the most nutritional benefit.

Flour

Wheat and other grains as nature made them are a nutritional plus. Most of the flour we use, however, has been refined, thus losing a great deal of its nutritional value in the process.

To appreciate what is lost in refining flour, it helps to know something about a kernel of grain as nature makes it. There are three main constituents in the whole-wheat kernel. Outermost is the *bran*—several layers of protective skin that consist primarily of fiber. The bran is lost when grains are refined. In a small area at the base of the kernel lies the *germ*—the embryo or sprouting section of the kernel—which contains vegetable oil (polyunsaturated fats), vitamins, and protein. Most of the kernel is the central *endosperm*, which is primarily starch, the food supply for the sprouting seed. The endosperm contains three-fourths of the protein in the wheat kernel and vitamins.

All the above constituents are found in whole-wheat flour that is stone-ground. Other methods of grinding whole-wheat flour lose somewhat more of the nutrients. Refined white flour is pure endosperm—both the bran and the germ have been removed and only about two thirds of the original kernel remains. Except for starch and protein, more than half of the essential nutrients in whole wheat are missing from white flour.

Most white flour sold in the United States has been "enriched," that is, some, but not all, of the vitamins and minerals removed during processing are added back. However, none of the natural fiber is replaced.

Bread

Despite the revival of interest in whole grains, three out of every four loaves of bread sold in America are white breads. You get the most nutrients for your money if you buy whole-grain bread made from stone-ground flour. The next best thing is 100-percent whole-wheat or other whole-grain bread. If you must buy white bread, at least make sure it's enriched.

All whole-wheat breads are brown, but not all brown breads are whole-wheat! By law, bread that is labeled "whole wheat" must be made from 100 percent whole-wheat flour. "Wheat bread" may be made from varying proportions of enriched white flour and whole-wheat flour. The type of flour present in the largest amount is listed first on the ingredient label. If you enjoy "brown bread," you should know that the brown color can be provided by molasses (a thick, sticky, brownish liquid produced when sugar is refined). Be sure to read the label. Buy ingredients, not color.

You don't have to switch to whole-wheat bread to increase your intake of whole grains. Many products on the market are made of a mixture of whole-grain flours and enriched flour. The following offer variety in taste and texture, as well as providing a bonus of fiber and nutrients: multi-grain bread, cracked-wheat bread, oat-meal bread, pumpernickel bread, rye bread, bran muffins, corn bread, and whole-wheat crackers.

Cereals

Cereals, particularly the "old-fashioned" kinds, can be the foundation of a nutritious breakfast. They can be eaten as snacks as well. Because they are made from grains, cereals are rich in complex carbohydrates and generally low in fat. Most cereals also provide a variety of vitamins, minerals, and healthy fiber. Unfortunately, many processed cereals have had unhealthy ingredients added to them, such as salt, fat, and refined sugar.

There is a wide variety of ready-to-eat and cooked cereals on the market. Faced with that diversity of products, shoppers looking for good nutrition as well as good taste can easily become confused—they often yield to advertising gimmicks and slogans such as "all natural," "no cholesterol," and "fortified with 100% of 10 essential

Helpful Tips

Choosing a Breakfast Cereal

The nutrition information on the package reveals much about the nutritional composition of the cereal. Here are some items for you to consider when choosing a cereal:

• *Serving size.* The usual serving size is 1 ounce of cereal, which can vary from 1/4 cup for granolas, to 1/2 cup for whole-bran cereals, to 1 cup for flake cereals, to 2 cups for some puffed cereals.

• *Calories per serving.* This ranges from about 70 (per 1-ounce serving) for whole-bran cereals to 150 for granolas.

• *The grain.* Look for a whole grain as the first ingredient listed. It can be whole wheat, whole rye, whole corn, oats, rice, or barley. Or it can be wheat bran, oat bran, or corn bran.

• *Dietary fiber.* You may find a listing for dietary fiber under "Carbohydrate Information" or a statement about fiber content somewhere else on the ingredient panel. Cereals made from bran are the highest in dietary fiber.

• *Fat.* Grains, the basis for most cereals, are naturally low in fat. For most cereals, the amount of fat per serving is only 1 or 2 grams, maybe 3 at the most. But watch out for granolas. True, they contain lots of nutritious goodies (such as nuts, seeds, and raisins), but they're also high in fats (from added oil plus the oil in the nuts and seeds), sugars, and calories. Granolas generally contain at least 5 grams of fat per serving. And often the fat is mostly saturated coconut or palm oil.

• *Sugar.* Avoid products in which sugar (or honey, corn syrup, fructose, or molasses) is listed as the first ingredient. This means that the product may contain over 50 percent sugar by weight (that's as much as 4 teaspoons of sugar in a 1-ounce serving!). Often, there is more than one source of sweetener,

Continued

so even if sugar is not listed as the first ingredient, there may still be more sugar in the cereal than anything else.

If a product has only a few ingredients, sugar or some other sweetener may appear near the top of the ingredients list even though the cereal may not contain much sugar. Therefore, it helps to check the "Carbohydrate Information" usually listed at the bottom of the ingredients panel. This listing separates the sugars from the nutritionally more desirable starches. Look for products that contain no more than 3 or 4 grams of "sucrose and other sugars" per serving.

• *Sodium.* Many cereals contain surprisingly large amounts of sodium, mostly from added salt. When milk is added, which naturally contains sodium, the total sodium per serving can exceed 400 milligrams. Hot cereals (like oatmeal and cream of wheat), when prepared without added salt, have less than 10 milligrams of sodium per serving, making them ideal for people on low-salt diets. If you choose "instant" hot cereals, be sure to read the label—many contain added salt.

• *Protein.* Among the commonly consumed grains, oats contain the most protein, corn and rice the least. Granolas that contain nuts and seeds may have more protein than ordinary flake cereals, but they also contain too many calories from fat and sugars. If you eat your cereal with a cup of low-fat or nonfat milk, you'll add 8 grams of high-quality protein.

• *Vitamins and minerals.* Fortification of cereals with vitamins and minerals is not in itself bad. But it is often used more to benefit sales than to improve the nutritional value of the product. Unless one serving of dry cereal is all you plan to eat for the rest of the day, there's no reason for your cereal to provide 100 percent of any one required nutrient, let alone 10 of them. Keep in mind, too, that no level of fortification can offset a high sugar or fat content, nor can it make up for all the nutrients lost when the grain is refined. It is always best to start with a whole-grain cereal.

vitamins." What is missing in these claims is the fact that these cereals are often high in sugar, salt, fat, and calories.

Fortunately, most cereal products carry nutrition information on the package label. Along with the ingredients list, this information can help you resist advertising pressures and choose products that will provide you with high nutritional value. As a general rule, the shorter the list of ingredients, the more nutritious the product.

Potatoes

Potatoes as they come from nature are a real nutritional bargain. In addition to vitamins, minerals, and trace nutrients, they also contain protein. But frying potatoes significantly changes the nutrient-to-calorie ratio, to your disadvantage. The high temperature of deep-frying destroys some of the vitamins, and the fat adds tremendously to the calories without enhancing the nutrient content. For instance, 70 percent of the calories in French fries are fat calories. Whereas a half-pound baked potato has about 170 calories, a half pound of fries has 620!

Rice, Corn, and Other Grains

Brown rice (rice without the bran removed) is the best choice among the different types of rice, because of its fiber content and nutritional value. White polished rice, the most popular type of rice in industrialized nations, has had the bran removed in the refining process, thereby losing some of its protein and much of its valuable vitamins and minerals. Parboiled or converted white rice retains more of the original nutrients because the process of parboiling forces some of the vitamins from the bran into the white endosperm. Instant and "minute" rice are the lowest in nutrient content.

Perhaps the most familiar form of corn to Americans is popcorn. Without butter or oil and with just a gentle sprinkling of salt, popcorn makes an excellent low-calorie, high-fiber snack food.

Pasta

Pasta is made from a hard spring wheat called durum, which is totally unsuitable for breads and cakes because it won't rise. The durum wheat is refined into a white flour called semolina, which is mixed with water and other ingredients to make a dough that can be cut into the desired shape. Semolina is about 15 percent protein, with a good balance of essential amino acids, and it has very little fat. Be sure to buy enriched products.

Meals that include pasta are easy to prepare and most nutritious as well. A variety of pasta is now available on the market, including whole-grain pasta, pasta made with vegetables (such as spinach), and pasta made with egg white (instead of the yolk).

Avoid high-fat, creamy sauces with your pasta. Instead, use low-fat sauces, such as marinara (made with tomatoes, onions, and garlic) or primavera (prepared with mixed vegetables).

Dried Beans and Peas

In vegetables like soybeans, kidney beans, pinto beans, navy beans, lentils, and black-eyed peas, the carbohydrates come packaged with a nutritional bonus—lots of high-quality protein. A cup of cooked soybeans contains 20 grams of protein, just a little bit less than a cup of ground beef. But the soybeans have half the calories—230 compared to 470 for the beef—and none of the saturated fat and cholesterol. (For more on dried beans and peas, see Chapter 9).

Fruits and Vegetables

Most fruits and vegetables are good sources of starch and natural sugars. The sugars come in a low-calorie package along with healthy supplies of vitamins, minerals, and indigestible fiber. Many vegetables contain small but significant amounts of protein as well. The fiber and water content of fruits and vegetables add satisfying bulk and volume to your diet and help prevent overeating. Fruits can satisfy that end-of-the-meal sweet craving in a nutritious, non-fattening way.

The most nutritious way to eat fruits and vegetables is raw. Fresh fruits and vegetables are richer sources of vitamins and minerals than fruits and vegetables that have been canned, since vital nutrients are lost during processing and storage. Frozen fruits and vegetables are almost as nourishing as fresh.

Milk Products

The bulk of calories in skim (nonfat) milk and many products made with skim or partially-skimmed milk is provided by carbohydrates. In skim milk, for example, nearly 60 percent of the calories come from carbohydrates—namely, the milk sugar lactose—and only 2 percent come from fat. On the other hand, in whole milk and products like cheese that are made from whole milk and cream, fats provide the bulk of calories. (For more on milk and dairy products, see Chapter 6).

And What about Sugar?

Sugars are found naturally in some foods. Most fruits and some vegetables contain sugars such as glucose, fructose, and sucrose. Another sugar, lactose, is found in milk and dairy products. Legumes and cereals contain small amounts of maltose. Besides sugars, these foods provide needed vitamins and minerals.

Unfortunately, a major portion of carbohydrates in the American diet today comes from refined or processed sugars, which are extracted from their natural sources and added to foods that do not naturally contain them. Processed foods (such as cookies, cakes, and candy) are rich in refined sugars and relatively low in nutrients. These foods contribute a large amount of calories without any important nutrients (in other words, "empty" calories).

"Sugar" means all forms of caloric sweeteners, including white sugar, brown sugar, raw sugar, corn syrup, honey, and molasses. By far our most widely used sugar is sucrose, extracted from sugar cane and beets. Sucrose is synonymous with white, refined table sugar. There's no real advantage of one type of sugar over another. Brown sugar, which is sucrose colored with a little molasses, and raw sugar, which is unrefined, are no more nourishing than white sugar. They are all "pure energy"—calories but no other nutrients of any significance.

Many Americans consume over 500 calories of sugar and other sweeteners each day, primarily from soft drinks, desserts, candy, jelly, and syrup. Even those who "don't eat sweets" probably consume far more sugar than they realize because so much of it is "hidden" in soft drinks and processed foods. A single 12-ounce can of soda pop, for example, contains 8 to 10 teaspoons of sugar, or about 140 "empty" calories. A tablespoon of ketchup contains a teaspoon of sugar.

There is little question that sugar in the diet promotes tooth decay. The occurrence of tooth decay depends not only on the amount of sugar eaten but also on the frequency and degree of stickiness of the sugar food. Sugar is also fattening—a lot of sugar calories can get packed into a rather small quantity of food. By eating sweets, people are more likely to over-consume calories long before they feel full, thus overloading the body with calories. Excess calories of any kind (whether from sugar, protein, or fat) are then stored as body fat.

For these reasons, it is suggested that you consume foods rich in sugar only occasionally, as a treat, rather than as part of your daily diet. The major portion of carbohydrates should be in the form of complex carbohydrates found in "starchy" foods, and naturally occurring sugars found in fresh fruits and some vegetables.

Should You Use Artificial Sweeteners?

Saccharin and aspartame (Nutrasweet™) are artificial sweeteners commonly used in diet beverages, tabletop sweeteners, and other products to provide sweetness without unwanted calories. One packet of aspartame, for example, is as sweet as two teaspoons of sugar (32 calories) but supplies only 4 calories.

Artificial sweeteners can be used to sweeten foods and beverages in which you would normally use table sugar. They can also be used in simple recipes that do not require heating. Since saccharin does not have the same baking characteristics as sugar, special recipes must be used for preparing baked products using this sweetener. Aspartame decomposes with heat and is not appropriate for baking purposes.

Most experts feel that it is not necessary to use artificial sweeteners to avoid too much sugar in the diet. First, these substances seem to perpetuate your craving for sweet foods. In addition, no artificial sweetener has ever been shown to help people

Cutting Down On Sugar

At the Supermarket

• Read the ingredients label. Sugars can be listed under a variety of names, such as: sugar, sucrose, glucose, dextrose, sorbitol, fructose, maltose, lactose, mannitol, honey, syrup (corn, maple, etc.), and molasses.

• If one of these sugars is listed as one of the first three ingredients, or if several sugars are listed on the label, the product is probably high in sugar. Don't worry about sugar as a minor ingredient in foods like soups or bread, or in condiments (like ketchup) eaten in small quantities.

• Buy fewer foods that are high in sugar, such as baked goods, candy, sweet desserts, soft drinks, and fruit-flavored punches. Don't buy sweet snacks or candy "to have in the house." Instead, keep a supply of fresh fruits and vegetables.

In the Kitchen

• Reduce the sugar in foods prepared at home. Try new recipes or adjust your own. Start by reducing the sugar gradually until you've decreased it by one-third or more.

• Experiment with spices such as cinnamon, cardamom, coriander, nutmeg, and ginger to enhance the flavor of foods.

At the Table

• Serve fresh fruit for desserts. If you must rely on canned or frozen fruit, look for brands that are packaged in water or their own juice, instead of sweetened syrup.

• Eat sweets only as an occasional treat. You may find that when you decide to limit sweets for a while (a week or longer), your craving for them gradually subsides.

Continued

• If you add sugar to your coffee, tea, or breakfast cereal, try gradually reducing the amount you use. Get used to adding half as much, then see if you can cut back even more.

• Use less of all sugars. This includes white and brown sugar, honey, molasses, and syrups.

• Cut back on the number of soft drinks, punches, and ades (lemonade, orangeade) you drink. This one measure could bring a significant reduction in the amount of sugar you consume. Instead, try club soda, seltzer, or mineral water, with a twist of lemon or lime.

• Choose ready-to-drink fruit juice from the can or bottle, or mixed from frozen concentrate with little or no added sugar. To get the most fruit juice with the least amount of added sugar, be sure the product label says fruit "juice," and not fruit "drink" or "-ade."

lose weight and keep it off. In fact, some people with the worst weight problems are among the heaviest saccharine and aspartame users, and many successful weight losers never used artificial sweeteners to help them lose weight and keep it off. Finally, questions concerning the safety of artificial sweeteners have been raised. So far, however, there is no definite indication that these substances can cause long-term harmful effects.

⑨ Dietary Fiber: From Apples to Oat Bran

Dietary fiber has been receiving increased attention as a crucial component of our diet. And that's pretty good for something that has no nutritional value of its own and is not even absorbed into the body! In this chapter you'll learn about the two types of fiber (soluble and insoluble) and their roles in keeping us healthy.

Dietary Fiber—Soluble and Insoluble

Dietary fiber has a chemical structure somewhat similar to that of starches (complex carbohydrates). Unlike starches, however, fiber is not broken down by digestive enzymes—its structure remains intact as it passes through the digestive tract. Fiber is not absorbed into the body and has no nutritional value of its own.

All fiber comes from plants—from cell walls that give plants their firm structure and from other nonstructured substances that are mixed with plant starches. There is no fiber in foods of animal sources such as meat, poultry, seafood, and dairy products. The most common sources of fiber in our diets are whole grains, fruits, and vegetables.

Based on their solubility (ability to dissolve) in water, dietary fiber can be grouped into two categories: soluble and insoluble. Oat bran, for example, has mainly soluble fiber, whereas wheat bran contains mostly insoluble fiber. Plants contain both types of fiber, in varying proportions. While the two types of fiber produce different effects in the body, they play equally important functions in maintaining health.

Soluble fibers, in the form of gluey gums and jelly-like pectins, disperse easily in water and form a bulky gel in the intestines during digestion. High intakes of soluble fiber have been reported to lower blood cholesterol levels by up to 15 percent. A significant amount of soluble fiber is found in oat bran and oat products, dried beans and peas, corn, barley, and some fruits and vegetables.

Insoluble fibers, which are derived from plant cell walls, trigger muscular action to increase intestinal regularity. They pass through the gastrointestinal system intact, adding bulk, absorbing water, and decreasing the time it takes foods to move through the digestive tract. Insoluble fibers act as a natural laxative and are useful in preventing constipation. They have very little or no effect on blood cholesterol levels. Good sources of insoluble fiber include unprocessed wheat bran, corn-bran and wheat-bran cereals, whole-wheat breads, dried peas and beans, seeds, popcorn, and most fruits and vegetables (best eaten with their skin).

Good Sources of . . .

Soluble Fiber

Oat bran	Black-eye peas	Green peas
Oatmeal	Kidney beans	Potato
Oat products	Navy beans	Zucchini
Cornmeal	Split peas	Apple
Barley	Corn	Pear
Oat cereals	Carrots	Prunes

Insoluble Fiber

Unprocessed bran	Graham crackers	Squash
Barley	Popcorn	Potato
Bran cereals	Dried beans & peas	Apple
Fiber cereals	Brussels Sprouts	Dried figs
Whole-wheat bread	Corn	Prunes
Bran muffins	Green peas	Raspberries

Soluble Fiber—It's Good for Your Heart

Studies have shown that in people with high blood cholesterol, a diet supplemented with oat bran or dried beans can reduce cholesterol levels by up to 15 percent. The cholesterol-lowering properties are related to the soluble fiber content of these foods.

Soluble fiber works primarily by binding to bile acids in the intestine, causing them to be eliminated in the stools. (Bile acids are substances manufactured in the liver from cholesterol, then released into the intestine to aid in fat digestion.) The more bile acids are lost, the more the liver has to make. The more bile acids are made, the more cholesterol is drawn out of the blood, and the lower the blood cholesterol level.

Although oat bran and dried beans deserve an important role in any cholesterol-lowering plan, there is nothing magical about either of these foods. It is the soluble fiber in them that causes cholesterol levels to go down, and any food (or combination of foods) that provides the same amount of soluble fiber can be expected to produce similar results.

So even though eating some oat bran and beans each day will make it easier for you to consume the amount of soluble fiber you need, you should not rely exclusively on them—or any other food—for this purpose. Other good sources of soluble fiber include grain products (bread, crackers, cereals), and a variety of fruits and vegetables. The greater the variety of foods you consume, the more interesting and nutritious your diet will be.

Oat Bran

Oat grains resemble a kernel of wheat in structure (see page 67). An outer covering of bran protects the starchy endosperm and the germ that is located at the bottom of the grain. The bran is the source of fiber, the endosperm is the source of energy, and the germ is the source of vitamins, minerals, and protein.

Old-fashioned rolled oats, normally referred to as *oatmeal*, are large, separate flakes that are produced from whole-grain oats. They contain oat bran. Old-fashioned rolled oats can be used in a wide range of recipes including cereals, main dishes, and desserts. Their normal cooking time is five minutes. *Quick rolled oats* are rolled oats that have been cut into pieces and preprocessed (heat-treated) for faster cooking. They cook in about one minute.

Instant oats are made from partly cooked, refined whole-grain oats and are rolled even thinner than quick oats. Their preprocessing often results in lack of nutrients, and they are usually packaged with sugar, salt, additives, and artificial flavorings. They are generally less nutritious and more expensive than old-fashioned and quick rolled oats.

When oat flakes are ground and sifted, the result is oat bran and oat flour. *Oat bran*, which has a pleasant, slightly nutty flavor, is made from the outer seed casing, or bran, of the whole-grain oat. The protein, vitamins, and minerals that are found naturally in oats are concentrated in the oat bran. Oat bran cooks in one to two minutes and can be served as a creamy, hot cereal or used as an ingredient in a wide variety of recipes. Oat-bran products are now available in most supermarkets and health-food stores. Oat bran can be eaten as a hot cereal, a cold cereal, or in muffins. Other baking options may include breads, rolls, cakes, and cookies.

Store-bought *oat flour* is produced by grinding whole-grain oats to a fine consistency. When it is milled to include oat bran, it is as nutritious as whole-grain oats. Oat flour can be blended with other flours for baking and used as a thickening agent for drinks, sauces, soups, and stews. Be sure that the oat flour you buy has been milled to include oat bran.

Integrating Oats into Your Diet

If you need to lower your cholesterol or want to be sure to maintain it at its current level, adding oats to your diet is a simple, safe, and natural way to move toward that goal. Studies have shown that your oat consumption will be more effective if you distribute it throughout the day. For instance, you may have a bowl of oat bran for breakfast, oat bran muffins as a part of your lunch, oat crust pizza for dinner, and a serving of oat cereal O's for a snack.

Oatmeal, like oat bran, is capable of lowering cholesterol levels. However, since oat bran is one part of the oat flake, it would take more oatmeal than oat bran to lower cholesterol to the same level.

Adding Fiber to Your Diet

• If you wish to increase the fiber content of your diet, do it gradually, over a period of weeks or months. Dietary fiber has a tendency to stimulate the formation of intestinal gas, and you may feel bloated if you suddenly start consuming large amounts of fiber.

• Incorporate the necessary changes into your current diet. This will allow you to consume more fiber without radically changing the way you currently eat. As the amount of high-fiber foods increases, the quantity of other foods will gradually decrease by itself.

• Provide your increased fiber from as large a variety of foods as possible. Don't focus on one or another type of fiber and neglect the rest. Whole grains may be the perfect cure for a sluggish intestine, and any type of fiber should help you control your weight.

• Be certain to drink lots of fluids when you increase the amount of fiber in your diet. Otherwise, fiber can be constipating instead of stimulating to your digestive system.

• When buying prepackaged grain cereals, breads, and other baked goods, be sure to read the label carefully. You don't want to negate the value of eating fiber by loading up on unnecessary saturated fats (such as coconut and palm oils), sugar, and salt.

• In general, coarse fiber is more effective than the same fiber ground fine. Look for the words "whole grain" or "whole wheat" when you buy breads or cereals.

• Fresh, raw fruits and vegetables have more useful fiber than those that have been peeled, cooked, pureed, or otherwise processed. Juices have little or no insoluble fiber. Some may, however, have soluble fiber.

For example, the benefit gained from consuming 1 ounce of oat bran would be equal to consuming 2 ounces of whole oats.

Introduce oats (or any other high-fiber food) into your daily eating plan on a slow, steady basis to avoid the possibility of increased intestinal gas and bloating. Be sure to eat a well-balanced diet to ensure the proper absorption of minerals (such as calcium, iron, magnesium, and zinc) into the bloodstream. And don't forget to drink plenty of liquids each day to avoid the possibility of constipation.

About Dried Beans and Peas

Dried beans and peas (like oat bran) have been shown to reduce blood cholesterol levels when included in the daily diet. Their cholesterol-lowering properties are related to their soluble fiber content. In addition to soluble fiber, dried beans and peas contain insoluble fiber as well, and so can be of great help in improving bowel function and promoting regularity.

In addition to fiber, these "nutritious wonders" come packaged with a healthy supply of complex carbohydrates, protein, vitamins, and minerals. They are very low in fat and of course, as plant foods, they contain no cholesterol. Dried beans and peas are richer in protein than any other plant foods. Although most contain "incomplete" proteins (see page 66), the deficiencies are easily overcome when beans and peas are eaten together with grains (such as corn, rice, wheat, and barley) or with a small amount of animal protein (such as meat, chicken, fish, or cheese).

Dried beans and peas, however, may cause some problems. First, they produce intestinal gas and bloating, which can be discomforting and sometimes even embarrassing. You should realize, however, that gas and bloating may be more of a problem for people who eat beans infrequently. This difficulty in digestion usually disappears in people who eat beans on a regular basis. You're likely to have less of a problem if you eat only a small amount of beans at any one time and don't mix them with other gas-producing vegetables such as cabbage. Or you can stick to the types of beans least likely to produce gas, such as lentils, black-eyed peas, lima beans, chickpeas, and white beans.

The other problem is that dried beans and peas take time to prepare—time to soak and time to cook. This can mean as much as an overnight soak plus an hour or two for cooking. So the time to think about making beans is anywhere from three hours to one day before you plan to eat them. An easy option is to buy already cooked beans and peas in cans or frozen packages. Keep a few cans of beans on hand for use in salads, soups, dips, and casseroles that you may want to make in a hurry. An alternative is to cook up a large batch of beans when you have the time and freeze the drained beans in meal-sized portions. Cooked beans, tightly covered, will keep for up to five days in the refrigerator.

Psyllium: The Laxative That Lowers Cholesterol

Psyllium is a soluble fiber sold as over-the-counter laxatives (such as Metamucil®). It comes from the husks of the seeds of the psyllium plant. Studies have shown that psyllium, when taken as a supplement to the diet, reduces blood cholesterol levels by up to 15 percent. Psyllium preparations are relatively safe. However, being a laxative, psyllium can cause gas, bloating, and intestinal upset. A number of cereal companies (such as Kellogg's and General Mills) have recently introduced new breakfast cereals containing a combination of bran and added psyllium.

Other Benefits of Dietary Fiber

Soluble fiber is not the only type of fiber found in foods of plant origin. As a matter of fact, most high-fiber foods (such as whole grains, fruits, vegetables, beans, nuts, and seeds) contain considerably more insoluble than soluble fiber.

As opposed to soluble fiber, the insoluble fraction has little or no effect on blood cholesterol. But it is an important part of your diet for a number of reasons: it provides bulk without calories; it is a part of foods which are high in healthy nutrients; and it has certain beneficial actions while it passes through the digestive tract.

A diet rich in fiber will provide enough bulk to keep your appetite under control while at the same time keeping your caloric

High Fiber Choices

Choose:	Instead of:
Whole-grain bread	White bread
Wheat or bran cereals	Highly processed cereals
Oat bran or oatmeal	Instant oatmeal
Bran muffins	Blueberry muffins
Brown rice	White rice
Popcorn	Potato chips
Unpeeled fruits	Peeled fruits
Fresh fruits	Fruit juices
Fresh fruit cup	Fruit-flavored sorbet
Fresh vegetables	Canned vegetables
Vegetable soup	Cream of mushroom soup
Baked potato (with skin)	Mashed potatoes
Whole-wheat pasta	Refined pasta
Kidney bean chili	Hamburger
Stir-fry vegetables	Sweet and sour pork

intake relatively low. In other words, you'll be able to eat less and still feel full. As a matter of fact, raw vegetables are now often served at many cocktail parties as an alternative to cold cuts, fried foods, cheese, and other high calorie foods. You can use this principle to lose weight and lower your cholesterol.

While fiber itself is not a nutrient, the company it keeps in most high-fiber foods results in a rich supply of essential nutrients. Fiber is found in whole grains, beans, fruits, and vegetables—all foods that are rich in complex carbohydrates, vitamins, and minerals. Beans, as we've mentioned, are also rich in protein. These fiber-rich foods are usually low in fat and contain no cholesterol. So, by eating high-fiber foods you'll not only get a rich supply of nutrients but also reduce your intake of fat and cholesterol.

One of the properties of fiber is that it traps water inside the digestive tract, thereby softening its contents. The result is that the muscular wall of the intestine works less and moves the intestinal contents more rapidly and at a lower pressure. In the short term, a high-fiber diet will result in a softening of the stool, which is very important particularly among older people where constipation is very common.

Several studies have shown that people who consume a diet rich in fiber and low in fat have a lower incidence of cancer of the colon (large intestine). So, in the long term, a high-fiber diet may reduce your risk for colon cancer. Of course, the earlier you start on a high-fiber diet, and the longer you adhere to it, the better.

How Much Fiber Should You Eat?

The average American consumes between 10 and 15 grams of dietary fiber a day (this is *total* fiber). Although experts are still debating the issue, most major health organizations recommend a diet that will provide somewhere between 25 and 35 grams of dietary fiber a day, with an upper limit of 40 grams. This amount of fiber should come from a variety of food sources such as whole grains, breads, cereals, fruits, and vegetables.

If you want to lower your cholesterol with dietary fiber, you should select foods that contain relatively large amounts of soluble fiber. Eating foods that are high in just total dietary fiber may not be enough, since the proportion of fiber that is soluble varies from food to food. Oat bran, for example, contains 48% soluble fiber, kidney beans contain 44%, apples contain 30%, and whole-wheat crackers only 20%. Taking these facts into account, a sound diet aimed at lowering cholesterol should contain somewhere between 10 and 15 grams of *soluble* fiber a day.

Most packaged high-fiber foods (such as breakfast cereals and breads) only have their *total* fiber content listed on the label. Many other high-fiber foods (grains, beans, fruits, and vegetables) don't

Guidelines:

A diet aimed at lowering cholesterol should contain between 10 and 15 grams of *soluble* fiber a day. The amount of *total* fiber should be between 25 and 35 grams, not to exceed 40 grams. This amount of fiber should come from a variety of food sources such as whole grains, breads, cereals, fruits, and vegetables.

come with labels at all, or the labels they have do not contain information about the fiber content. So how can you tell which foods have the most soluble fiber?

An easy way for you to determine the amount of fiber in the foods you eat is to refer to the fiber content table, in the appendix. There, you'll find both the amount of total fiber and the amount of soluble fiber contained in various foods, in grams per serving. Simply check the list and select the foods that you like that will help you meet your needs for soluble fiber. Obviously, choosing foods that are particularly rich in soluble fiber (such as oat products and beans) will make it easier for you to reach your goal.

10 Losing Weight and Keeping It Off

Obesity is an independent risk factor for heart disease. This means that people who are obese are more likely to develop coronary heart disease, even if they have no other risk factors. Not only does obesity alone contribute to heart disease, it is associated with other risk factors as well. Obese people, for example, are nearly three times as likely to have high blood pressure as people of normal weight. They are also more apt to have high blood cholesterol and diabetes.

Fortunately, obesity and related risk factors can be controlled by a program of weight loss and regular exercise. If you are obese, losing those extra pounds will help you keep your blood pressure under control. It will also help you lower your LDL-cholesterol ("bad" cholesterol), and raise your HDL-cholesterol ("good" cholesterol). In fact, if your blood cholesterol level is not too high, weight loss combined with other changes in your eating habits may be the only treatment you will ever need to control your cholesterol.

About Weight Gain and Weight Loss

Being obese simply means that you carry too much fatty tissue in your body. In terms of numbers, it means that you weigh 20 percent more than your desirable (or ideal) body weight. Your desirable weight is how much you should weigh, based on your height and body frame (build). To determine your desirable weight, refer to the height and weight chart, next page.

Height		Body frame		
feet	inches	small	medium	large
Men				
5	1	123-129	126-136	133-145
5	2	125-131	128-138	135-148
5	3	127-133	130-140	137-151
5	4	129-135	132-143	139-155
5	5	131-137	134-146	141-159
5	6	133-140	137-149	144-163
5	7	135-143	140-152	147-167
5	8	137-146	143-155	150-171
5	9	139-149	146-158	153-175
5	10	141-152	149-161	156-179
5	11	144-155	152-165	159-183
6	0	147-159	155-169	163-187
6	1	150-163	159-173	167-192
6	2	153-167	162-177	171-197
6	3	157-171	166-182	176-202
Women				
4	9	99-108	106-118	115-128
4	10	100-110	108-120	117-131
4	11	101-112	110-123	119-134
5	0	103-115	112-126	122-137
5	1	105-118	115-129	125-140
5	2	108-121	118-132	128-144
5	3	111-124	121-135	131-148
5	4	114-127	124-138	134-152
5	5	117-130	127-141	137-156
5	6	120-133	130-144	140-160
5	7	123-136	133-147	143-164
5	8	126-139	136-150	146-167
5	9	129-142	139-153	149-170
5	10	132-145	142-156	152-173
5	11	135-148	145-159	155-176

Chart 6. Desirable weights for adults age 25 and older (weight in pounds, without clothing).

Being overweight does not just happen overnight—it creeps up on us gradually. Most people do not deliberately overeat. But they become overweight from those extra calories they unthinkingly consume each day. A daily excess of only 200 calories, for example, may lead in the course of a year to the build-up of almost 20 pounds of fatty tissue.

Also, as we mature we begin to need fewer calories than we needed during our active growing years. With every year past age 25 our caloric needs drop by about one percent a year. Most of us, however, tend to keep on eating as much or almost as much as we did during our youth. Extra weight then becomes noticeable in women in their thirties and in men in their forties.

"Fad" diets that promise a quick and easy way to lose weight have always been popular, because it is easier to follow a diet than it is to change old eating habits. Such diets usually lead to failure because these methods of reducing are based on the assumption that losing weight is a temporary, short-term matter. Also, fad diets that emphasize one category of food and promise rapid weight loss can cause a chemical imbalance in the body and may result in dangerous medical conditions.

The basic principle of weight gain is simple: people gain weight because they consume more calories (whether from carbohydrate, protein, or fat) than their body burns. Therefore, the only way to lose weight is by creating a negative caloric balance, that is, by expending (burning) more calories than are being consumed. This can be achieved through reduction of caloric intake or through increase of caloric expenditure, or a combination of both. In other words, the answer to the problem of obesity is to eat less, eat properly, and exercise more!

Remember:

The only sure way to lose weight is to take in fewer calories than you burn—by eating less, eating properly, and exercising more.

Assessing Your Eating Habits

Begin your weight loss effort by becoming more aware of the way you eat now. Take a critical look at your eating habits. At what times of the day do you usually eat? Do you routinely skip some meals? At what time do you eat the largest meal? Where do you eat (in a restaurant, a cafeteria at work, fast-food restaurant, a deli, at home, or in the homes of others)? Are meals eaten at home prepared from packaged foods or fresh from the market? Which are your favorite foods and what foods do you dislike? What foods will be most difficult to eat more, or less of?

Without changing your current diet, keep a record of everything you eat and drink for a period of three days. In your record, note what, when, where and how much you consume. Also, write down briefly with whom you were eating and how you were feeling at the time (hungry, bored, tired, lonely, etc.). Such a record will give you information about the type and amount of foods you eat. It will also provide information about your behavior—the why, when, and where of eating. Because eating is something we do every day, the way we eat is largely habit.

After gathering this information, take an objective look at the type and amount of foods and drinks on your record. Pay special attention to the serving sizes of fatty foods, snacks, rich desserts, and alcohol, since these are "calorie-dense" foods. Does your diet contain a healthy variety of foods? Does it contain at least 5 servings of fruits and vegetables daily? Do you consume 2 servings of low-fat or nonfat dairy products each day? If the answer is no, now is the time to plan changes in these areas.

Next, decide which foods you can omit or decrease to cut your intake. It may be appropriate to remove fatty meats, snacks, and desserts from your diet. In general, it's easier and more effective to reduce rather than totally eliminate certain foods.

Skipping meals is seldom effective in reducing caloric intake. People who skip breakfast and lunch become so hungry that they start snacking in mid-afternoon and don't stop eating until bedtime. Regular meals and snacks are a better way to help control your appetite and give you a constant source of energy.

Helpful Tips

Changing Your Eating Habits

• Plan a balanced diet around familiar foods. Choose lower calorie foods and lower calorie ways of food preparation. Don't forget to include fresh vegetables and fruits at every meal—they are low in calories and high in bulk.

• Be aware of the number of calories in the foods you eat. Study the food tables in the appendix to familiarize yourself with foods that are unexpectedly rich in calories.

• Try to eat three meals a day at fairly regular times. Eat only at the kitchen table or dining-room table, at a place that has been set with silverware and a plate.

• Don't skip meals. Skipping breakfast and lunch is usually compensated by a heavy dinner. Skipping meals also lowers your resistance to snacking between times. You may end up consuming more calories than if you had eaten a real meal.

• Budget your calories to take care of snacks, weekend eating, and holidays. Plan ahead for special occasions by eating less at breakfast and lunch.

• Go grocery shopping after you've eaten a satisfying meal. If you shop when you're hungry, you are likely to select more fattening foods than you otherwise would. Do not buy foods that are likely to be tempting or high in calories.

• Let your family and friends know that you're trying to cut down. Ask them not to offer you seconds or urge you to eat when you say "no, thanks." Ask them to help by not tempting you with foods you love.

• Limit your alcohol consumption, and stay away from high-calorie mixers and sweet liqueurs. Ounce per ounce, alcohol has nearly as many calories as fat. Instead of a refill, try plain soda or mineral water with a wedge of lemon or lime.

Continued

• Don't let an occasional indulgence be an excuse for going completely overboard. If you have "blown" your diet, you can make up for it by cutting back a little the next day, or by getting some extra exercise.

• If certain activities or times of day are associated with between-meal eating, change your routine. Walk the dog after dinner instead of sitting down in front of the TV set with a can of peanuts.

• Don't weigh yourself more than once or twice a week while you're trying to lose. Losing fat takes time, and you may get discouraged if you don't see daily progress on the scale.

• "Diet" food doesn't have to be tasteless and boring. Instead of high-calorie fats, oils, and dressings, season your foods generously with herbs and spices. Experiment a little until you find combinations you especially like.

• Depriving yourself of your favorite treats will only make you want them more. Plan to enjoy a small portion of these "forbidden" treats once or twice a week.

• Seeing foods can stimulate your desire to eat. At home, store tempting items in the back of the cupboard so they're harder to see and reach. Put leftovers in opaque containers so you don't see them every time you open the refrigerator.

• A sensible program of regular exercise, preferably every day, should become an integral part of your weight-control program.

• Make exercise part of your daily activities. Walk whenever possible. Use the stairs for a few flights instead of taking the elevator. Regular exercise tones muscles, improves circulation, and helps you lose fat without getting flabby.

• Finally, remember that you're changing habits, that this process takes time. Start small and keep trying. The new habits you form will be well worth the effort.

Developing Your Awareness for Calories

The energy value of foods is measured in units of heat energy, or calories. To maintain a constant level of body weight, the number of calories you consume each day must balance the number of calories you burn each day. If you consume more calories than your body requires, the excess calories are stored as body fat.

The number of calories you need each day to meet your energy expenditures is your "daily caloric needs." This value depends on several factors, including your desirable body weight, your activity level, and your gender. To determine your daily caloric needs, refer to chart 4, on page 55.

If you want to overcome a weight problem, you must develop your awareness of the caloric "cost" of foods and learn to regulate your daily intake of calories. The healthy approach to losing weight is to choose a variety of foods with the nutrients you need, and go easy on foods that supply mainly calories (such as fatty meats, snacks, desserts, and alcoholic beverages).

You must also cultivate your sense of estimating portion sizes, because if you eat a larger portion of the recommended food, you won't be saving the calories you should.

Certain foods (like bread, potatoes) are thought of as "fattening" while others (like cottage cheese, meat) are believed to be good for losing weight. There is no truth to these beliefs. Foods that contain a large number of calories contribute to weight gain while foods containing fewer calories make weight loss possible.

Three nutrients provide the calories in foods—carbohydrates, proteins, and fats. All foods contain a combination of these three nutrients plus water. As we already know, fats contribute twice as many calories as either carbohydrates or protein. If there's a food that's truly "fattening," it's fat!

Foods high in fat are often described as "calorie dense." You get a lot of calories from a small volume of food. For example, one tablespoon of butter or margarine contains 120 calories, a tablespoon of sugar contains 50 calories, and a tablespoon of apple sauce contains only 10 calories.

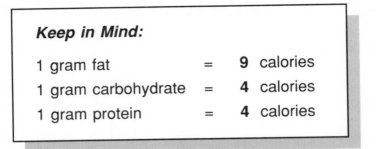

Keep in Mind:

1 gram fat	=	**9**	calories
1 gram carbohydrate	=	**4**	calories
1 gram protein	=	**4**	calories

Calorie-dense foods have another disadvantage, especially for people who eat rapidly. Quick eaters can consume a large quantity of high-fat, calorie-dense foods such as nuts, candy bars, or potato chips in a short period of time. If instead they ate foods with lower caloric density such as fruits, vegetables, or even grain products, the same volume of food would provide far fewer calories.

In figuring how much you consume, don't neglect to include the caloric contribution of alcoholic beverages. Ounce for ounce, alcohol has more calories than either carbohydrates or protein and nearly as much as fat. If you're serious about losing weight, limit yourself to one drink a day (or none) and stay away from high-calorie mixers and sweet liqueurs.

Beware of "hidden" fat, a concentrated source of calories. Some foods we ordinarily think of as highly nourishing and good diet foods are actually loaded with fat. These include hard cheeses, nuts and seeds, granola cereals, and most meats. Peanut butter, avocados, and canned tuna (packed in oil) are also rich in fat.

Achieving and Maintaining a Desirable Weight

In order to lose weight, you must take in fewer calories than your body burns. The most practical diet consists of foods you like, tailored to your needs. The greatest reduction should be in calorie-dense foods such as fats, fatty meats, snacks, desserts, and alcohol. Another way to reduce calories is to take smaller portions of all foods in your diet.

At the Table

• Restrict all your eating to one or two places (such as the kitchen and dining-room tables) in your home. This helps reduce the number of places you associate with food.

• For everything you eat, whether it's a full-course dinner or just coffee and toast, set yourself a place with a napkin and utensils and sit down to eat it. This will help your mind identify this as a meal. Seeing the food on a plate also helps you realize how much you're consuming.

• Don't watch television or read the newspaper while you eat. Instead, concentrate on your meal. This will make the meal more satisfying and will help you eat less.

• Serve yourself on a smaller plate. Smaller portions will fill your plate up and you're less likely to feel deprived by relatively small servings.

• Eat sensible portions. Don't eat "family style," with the serving dishes on the table. Serve from the stove or refrigerator and put away the leftovers as soon as you've taken what you consider a reasonable portion.

• Eat slowly. Learn to stop eating before you feel full. Give your stomach and brain a chance to realize they've had enough, before you get to the second or third helping.

• When dining out, practice portion control. Most restaurants give servings that are far larger than you would dish up for yourself at home. You don't have to finish it all. Offer some to a tablemate or take some home in a "doggie bag."

• If the regular dinner comes with four or more courses and you know it's going to add up to more food than you want or need, order à la carte. Order an appetizer and salad, or share a dinner with someone and get an extra salad or appetizer.

Obviously, the lower your caloric intake, the more rapid your weight loss. However, rapid or excessive weight loss may result in a variety of symptoms such as weakness, dizziness, hair loss, skin changes, cold intolerance, constipation, and depression. Also, very low-calorie diets are likely to be short-term. You may tolerate a severe diet restriction for a while, but you'll eventually give in to hunger and the limits on your lifestyle. If you are severely obese and must lose a large amount of weight rapidly, it is imperative that you get a complete medical evaluation and that you follow a diet under the supervision of a physician.

If you need to lose weight, a sensible approach and a moderate loss of 1 to 2 pounds per week is recommended. As a rule of thumb, a reduction in food intake equivalent to 3,500 calories will result in a weight loss of 1 pound. Thus, by consuming 500 fewer calories a day, you could lose 1 pound per week.

If, for example, you normally burn 2,000 calories a day, you can theoretically expect to lose a pound of fat each week if you adhere to a 1,500-calorie-a-day diet. You could do the same by burning up 500 calories per day through exercise.

Whether you follow a diet prescribed by a physician, a registered dietitian, or a weight-reduction group is a matter of personal choice. You may find it easier to diet with a group, since this often helps to boost motivation by providing peer support. Weight reduction programs (such as Weight Watchers®) offer sensible, well-balanced diet plans, plus plenty of tips and moral support.

As we've seen, it is important to increase caloric expenditure in order to burn excess body fat. This can be achieved by regular exercise. There is no need to start a strenuous exercise program or to become an "exercise nut" in order to put some regular activity back into your life. Energy can be expended by integrating some sort of physical activity during the course of a day, such as walking instead of riding, climbing a few flights of stairs instead of taking the elevator, and leaving the car at the far end of the lot instead of parking right in front of the store.

Even if you succeed in losing a few pounds on a reducing diet, chances are you will gain the weight back unless you change your

The Healthy Way to Snack

• If you have a tendency to snack because you are bored, plan an activity or get involved in a hobby that you can turn to instead of eating. Know your most vulnerable times for nibbling, and plan activities for those times.

• Plan your own snacks for a certain time of day and prepare them ahead. Stock up on low-calorie substitutes. Cut up a bag full of fresh vegetables or a bowl of fresh fruit and set it aside, ready for consumption.

• One way to get in several snacks during the day without adding extra calories to your diet is to save parts of your meals to eat as snacks later on. Appetizer, dessert, and salad are ideal for this purpose.

• When you are eating a snack, don't do anything else. Don't watch television, read the paper, or talk on the phone. The idea is to dissociate eating from other activities so that you won't think of food when you're doing other things.

• Don't eat foods (chips and crackers, for instance) out of boxes or bags. This leads to eating more than you want or need since you can't judge how much you've eaten until your fingers hit the bottom of the container!

• Limit or avoid high-calorie snacks such as crackers, potato chips, nuts, cookies, candies, or chocolate. Don't keep high-calorie snack foods around the house "just in case" unexpected guests drop in.

• Some good choices in snacks are graham crackers, rye krisp, Melba toast, soda crackers, bagels, English muffins, ready-to-eat cereals (watch out for granolas), fresh fruits, and raw vegetables. Popcorn should be air popped or cooked in small amounts of liquid vegetable oil.

> **Remember:**
>
> • The healthy approach to losing weight is to eat a variety of foods containing the nutrients you need, and go easy on foods that supply mostly calories.
>
> • A sensible approach with a moderate loss of 1 to 2 pounds a week is best. A rapid or excessive weight loss may result in a variety of health problems, and is more likely to be short-term.
>
> • It is important that you increase your caloric expenditure in order to burn off excess body fat. You can do that by exercising regularly and integrating some physical activity into the course of your day.

eating habits at the same time. Behavior modification is a method that deals directly with the underlying cause of obesity, namely, your eating behavior. It focuses on changing your eating habits so that weight loss may be maintained on a long-term basis. Behavior modification does not promise a shortcut to successful weight loss, and it is neither quick nor especially easy. Rather it emphasizes gradual weight loss and provides new eating habits that will help maintain the loss indefinitely.

You must realize that permanent weight loss cannot be achieved overnight. Those extra pounds you carry were not acquired in a few weeks or months. Chances are, they've accumulated gradually over a period of years. While you probably can get rid of these extra pounds faster than they were acquired, you should give yourself a chance to learn a new way to deal with food, a new behavior that will help you control your caloric intake and keep those extra pounds off for years to come.

11 Exercising Your Way to a Healthier Heart

Although more people than ever before are aware of the benefits of exercise and participate in various types of recreation, many still do not get enough physical activity. Modern society encourages a sedentary lifestyle. Most people drive to work and to stores, use elevators instead of stairs, are spectators rather than participants in sporting activities, and do little heavy labor on their jobs.

The Benefits of Exercise

Several studies have shown a statistical link between a sedentary lifestyle and increased incidence of heart disease. Other investigations have shown, although not conclusively, that an exercise training program may decrease the chances of getting a heart attack. Regular exercise also has a positive effect on other risk factors: it tends to lower blood pressure, helps control weight, and increases the level of HDL-cholesterol ("good" cholesterol). In addition, many smokers give up the habit once they start exercising.

Regular exercise results in "conditioning" of the cardiovascular system, by improving the efficiency of oxygen utilization by the heart, lungs, and body muscles. Cardiovascular fitness is a state of body efficiency that enables a person to exercise for longer periods of time without excessive fatigue. The physically fit person is able to supply more energy to his muscles so that they can work harder and longer, and with less effort. Regular exercise also improves muscle tone and flexibility.

Regular exercise promotes the development of small new blood vessels within the heart muscle, termed "collateral circulation." This provides better blood flow to the heart muscle. Such blood vessels could potentially serve as emergency short-circuits and compensate for the loss in blood supply in case of a blockage of a coronary artery (heart attack).

Besides reducing the risk of heart disease and improving cardiovascular fitness, exercise provides several other benefits. It enhances a person's sense of well-being, helps release tension, and promotes relaxation and better sleep. Regular exercise also helps in coping with stress, anxiety, and depression. People who exercise regularly tend to be more energetic, enthusiastic, and optimistic.

Before You Start

It is true that most people will have no problem with a gradual and sensible exercise program. For some people, however, exercise can be dangerous. In fact, as many as 10 percent of apparently healthy adults over the age of 40 have heart problems they may not be aware of.

If you are over 40, especially if you are not accustomed to vigorous exercise, you should consult your doctor and undergo a medical checkup prior to starting an exercise program. You should also be checked if you are under 40 but have a history of heart disease or cardiac symptoms, have one or more major risk factors, or a family history of premature heart disease. (For a more complete checklist, see chart on facing page).

Depending on the information obtained during the medical checkup, your doctor may recommend an exercise stress test (treadmill). During the test, he or she will have you walk on a motor-driven treadmill while your heart rhythm and blood pressure are being monitored. This "road test" is used primarily to uncover the presence of hidden heart problems. It is also used to assess your level of cardiovascular fitness in order to design a fitness program that's right for you.

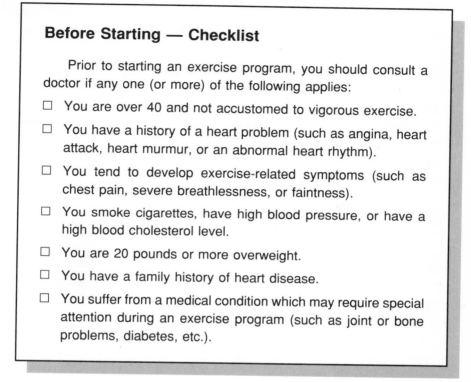

Before Starting — Checklist

Prior to starting an exercise program, you should consult a doctor if any one (or more) of the following applies:

☐ You are over 40 and not accustomed to vigorous exercise.

☐ You have a history of a heart problem (such as angina, heart attack, heart murmur, or an abnormal heart rhythm).

☐ You tend to develop exercise-related symptoms (such as chest pain, severe breathlessness, or faintness).

☐ You smoke cigarettes, have high blood pressure, or have a high blood cholesterol level.

☐ You are 20 pounds or more overweight.

☐ You have a family history of heart disease.

☐ You suffer from a medical condition which may require special attention during an exercise program (such as joint or bone problems, diabetes, etc.).

The Ingredients of a Good Exercise Program

When designing an exercise program, the key ingredients include: the type of activity; the intensity, duration, and frequency of the exercise; and the warm-up and cool-down periods.

Type of Physical Activity

Not all types of exercise promote cardiovascular fitness. Only those exercises which significantly increase the continuous flow of blood through the heart, lungs, and large muscles are beneficial. These exercises are termed "dynamic." Walking, swimming, and bicycling are dynamic exercises—they require continuous movement of the legs and arms, resulting in rhythmic tensing and relaxing of muscles, thus helping the flow of blood. Weight lifting, on the other hand, is not a dynamic activity—it causes the muscles being strengthened to tense up, therefore squeezing the blood vessels, and letting less blood pass instead of more.

Some types of exercise enhance blood flow but do not improve cardiovascular fitness, because they cannot be kept up for a sufficiently long period of time. So, the second requirement for the right type of exercise is that it must be capable of being sustained— it must be *aerobic* (meaning "with oxygen"). An aerobic exercise steadily supplies enough oxygen to the exercising muscles for as long as the exercise is continued.

Any rhythmic, repetitive, dynamic activity which can be continued for two or more minutes, without gasping for air afterwards, is probably aerobic. Sprinting is not an aerobic exercise—the sprinter cannot keep going at that pace for more than a minute or so. By contrast, the experienced jogger can cover long distances almost effortlessly, because his body has attained a balance between the oxygen it needs and the oxygen it is getting through the lungs and cardiovascular system.

Good aerobic exercises include brisk walking, jogging, running, bicycling, swimming, cross-country skiing, skating, tennis (singles), "aerobics" workouts, and jumping rope.

Exercises which are not considered aerobic include bowling, golf, weight lifting, down-hill skiing, tennis doubles, baseball, and volleyball. Although some of these exercises may seem strenuous, the level of activity usually is not sustained long enough to be aerobic—they do not improve endurance or "wind." Of course, types of exercise which do not improve cardiovascular fitness may have other benefits, such as gaining muscle strength, increasing body flexibility, and improving athletic skills.

Intensity, Duration, and Frequency

Cardiovascular conditioning occurs when a particular program involves an aerobic activity performed at an intensity level within the "target zone" (see below), for a duration of 20 to 30 minutes per session, and at a frequency of 3 to 4 times a week.

The maximum heart rate is the highest level a person's pulse can reach. You can estimate your maximum heart rate by subtracting your age from 220. To condition your heart and lungs, you must bring your heart rate (measured by taking your pulse) to a certain level, called the *target heart rate*, which depends on your age and on how far you have advanced in your exercise program.

Exercising below 60 percent of the maximum heart rate gives the heart and lungs little if any conditioning effect. Anything above 85 percent, on the other hand, adds little benefit for a great deal of extra exercise, and can be potentially dangerous. The area between the 60-percent and 85-percent levels is known as the *target zone*—the goal for which one should strive in order to improve cardiovascular fitness. (See chart 7, below).

The numerical values for the maximum heart rate and the target zone are only average values based on one's age. As many as one third of the population may differ from these values. For example, a healthy 60-year-old person may have a maximum heart rate of 180,

Age	Target Zone, 60-85% (beats per minute)	Average Maximum Heart Rate (100%)
20	120 - 170	200
25	117 - 166	195
30	114 - 162	190
35	111 - 157	185
40	108 - 153	180
45	105 - 149	175
50	102 - 145	170
55	99 - 140	165
60	96 - 136	160
65	93 - 132	155
70	90 - 128	150

Chart 7. The target zone heart rates, according to age

which is higher than expected at this age. A 30-year-old person, on the other hand, may have a maximum heart rate of only 170.

If you plan to start an exercise program, be aware that some medications and medical conditions can affect your maximum heart rate and target zone values. Some drugs taken for the treatment of high blood pressure (beta blockers), for example, may slow your pulse rate and lower your target zone. If you are currently taking cardiac medications, you should consult your doctor to determine whether your heart rate values should be adjusted.

You can determine whether you are within your target zone by taking your pulse immediately after the exercise activity. Place two or three fingers *lightly* over the carotid artery (located on either side of the neck), count the pulse for 10 seconds, and then multiply that number by 6 (this will give you the pulse rate per minute). Another convenient spot for checking the pulse is at the wrist, just below the base of the thumb.

At the beginning of the program, you may want to exercise at only 60 percent of your maximum heart rate, and then gradually increase the intensity over a period of several weeks or months. If you've been sedentary for an extended period of time, it may be wise for you to wait several months before raising your heart rate above the 70 percent level.

In order to provide a conditioning effect, the exercise session should last 20 to 30 minutes. If you are out of shape or have trouble sustaining exercise at target zone intensity for that long, you can adjust the duration of exercise. You may, for example, begin exercising at a target zone intensity for only 5 or 10 minutes a session, then gradually build up duration. Alternating exercise of high intensity and low intensity (such as jogging and walking) is another good way to start.

The optimal frequency for exercise is 3 or 4 times a week. Although the training effect on the body increases somewhat if the exercise is done more frequently, so does the chance of joint and muscle injury, particularly with exercises like jogging and running. If your exercise program consists mostly of walking or swimming (risk of injury is small), or if you exercise for weight control, you may want to increase the frequency, up to a daily schedule.

Warm-up and Cool-down Periods

Often overlooked is the importance of the warm-up and cool-down periods. The *warm-up period* helps stretch and loosen up the body muscles. It also stimulates the circulation, increases the heart rate, and prepares the cardiovascular system for the aerobic phase of the exercise session. A 5-minute warming up period will reduce your risk of muscle or joint injury, and will prevent the possibility of abruptly overtaxing your heart.

You should begin the warm-up with undemanding exercises, such as swinging the arms, and gently stretching the back, neck, and legs. Emphasis should be given to stretching the backs of the legs (hamstring and calf muscles). Your warm-up may then become more dynamic, perhaps with slow walking, jumping jacks, or running in place.

Equally important is the *cool-down period*. During a vigorous workout, blood vessels in the extremities become dilated as more blood and oxygen are supplied to the exercising muscles. When you stop, the blood vessels remain dilated, resulting in a "pooling" of blood in the extremities, thereby dropping the amount of blood pumped by the heart. This explains why abruptly stopping vigorous exercise can result in dizziness or even fainting. A 5-minute cooling down period allows a gradual slowing of the heart rate and a safer recovery. Cool-down activities generally consist of a brief relaxed walk and some stretching of the body and extremities.

Choosing an Exercise Program That's Right for You

When selecting a specific exercise program, you should consider the following factors: your health and physical capabilities, the equipment and facilities required, the weather and seasonal variability, your schedule, and last but not least, your own interests and preferences.

The activity you choose should provide enough exercise to get your body functioning at the target heart rate for a period of at least 20 to 30 minutes per session. The exercise should be demanding but not exhausting, and need not become competitive. The type of exercise should provide you with some pleasure and enjoyment—it should be an activity that interests you enough so you can continue with it for years to come.

Brisk walking is by far the most convenient form of exercise. This enjoyable activity can be performed almost anywhere, it is the easiest to fit into a hectic daily routine, it can easily be done alone or in a group, and it requires no athletic skill or talent. It is also the easiest to monitor with respect to pulse rates, time, and distance. Walking appeals particularly to people for whom more strenuous activities are either unappealing or medically ill-advised.

Jogging and *running* offer the most intense aerobic workout in the shortest amount of time, and provide an efficient way for getting lower-body muscular conditioning. Jogging is popular because it can be done almost anywhere, and requires no special equipment other than comfortable shoes. Jogging is recommended for people with healthy knees and feet. People who do not warm up properly and those who begin to run excessive distances risk muscle and joint injuries. You can start with the walking program for several weeks, then gradually ease into the jogging program, by alternating periods of walking and jogging within the same exercise session.

Swimming involves all of the major muscles in the body and it therefore gives more of a total conditioning effect than many other sports. Just paddling about or floating in the water, however, is not enough for cardiovascular conditioning! The real benefit of swimming will come only when you can swim lap after lap effortlessly for 20 minutes or more. Swimming is an excellent activity for obese individuals and for those who have leg joint problems or who have incurred injuries in other sports.

Many consider *bicycling* more fun than walking or jogging. Bicycling, though, is not as aerobic as jogging or running. It is almost exclusively a lower-body activity, thus helpful in conditioning leg muscles. Like swimming, it is a non-weight bearing activity, and is therefore a terrific choice for anyone with chronic joint or foot problems. There is relatively little danger of serious muscle and joint injury. (Injuries may result, however, from accidental encounters with the road, motorists, or other cyclists).

Helpful Tips

Precautions for Exercising Safely

Many exercise-related risks and injuries can be prevented by taking proper precautions. Here are some guidelines:

• Set realistic goals! Don't push yourself into doing too much too soon. Start slowly and increase speed, distance, and duration gradually. An optimal training goal is 75 percent of your maximum heart rate.

• Listen to your body! If you develop muscle and joint pains, you are probably progressing too fast. Don't make the mistake of exercising beyond these early warning signs, since more serious injuries may result.

• Warm up thoroughly prior to the workout, to stretch the muscles and tendons, and to stimulate the circulation. Cool down properly following the workout to allow the body to recover gradually.

• Stop exercising if you feel lightheaded, breathless, nauseated, or overly tired. Stop exercising and call your doctor if during or following exercise you develop pain in your chest or arms, a cold sweat, extreme breathlessness, faintness, or palpitations (skipped beats or "fluttering" in the chest).

• Use proper clothing. Don't overdress for exercise in warm or hot weather. Use proper equipment and facilities.

• Drink water before and after exercising, especially on a hot day. Avoid exercise on very hot and humid days (when temperature is above 90°F or humidity is above 80 percent).

• Wait at least two hours after a heavy meal before exercising, and at least four hours after consuming alcohol.

• Finally, take proper precautions to avoid automobile injuries. If walking or jogging in the dark (or when it's not fully light), wear light-colored clothes or a reflecting band, so that drivers can see you. Face oncoming traffic.

Stationary bicycles provide the convenience of use at home, even during poor weather. Most modern stationary bicycles are equipped with a speedometer and resistance controls, allowing easy monitoring of the exercise workload. Exercise equipment that simulates cross-country skiing is now becoming popular.

"Aerobics" workouts have become very popular in recent years. Aerobics is one of the more enjoyable and exciting activities, combining exercise, dance steps, and music. It can be performed either in large groups or in the privacy of your home. It can be done at your own pace. To obtain cardiovascular benefits, you should exercise at an intensity level that raises your heartbeat to within the target heart rate, and for at least 20 minutes.

. . . . . .

The various types of aerobic exercise are not equal in their capacity to induce cardiovascular fitness. The number of calories burned varies with the activity in question. Following are a few examples of caloric expenditures for selected physical activities, based on an average body size of 150 pounds.

Type of Activity	Cals. Burned / Hour
Walking, 2 to 4 mph	200 - 400
Jogging, 5 to 7 mph	500 - 800
Running, 8 to 10 mph	900 - 1200
Cycling, 6 mph	250 - 300
Cycling, 12 mph	400 - 500
Swimming, breast stroke	300 - 600
Swimming, crawl	600 - 900
Aerobics workout	300 - 500
Tennis, singles	400 - 500

Chart 8. Calories burned for selected physical activities

Is It Safe to Exercise?

You may have read or heard about people who during, or just after exercising, have a heart attack or experience sudden death. You may wonder, then, whether vigorous exercise is really safe. Before attempting to answer this important question, several comments should be made.

First of all, the actual risk of suffering a massive heart attack or dying as a result of vigorous exercise is very small. Out of hundreds of thousands of people who exercise each day, the reported cases of sudden death are extremely rare.

Second, the cardiac event may not necessarily be the result of the exercise activity itself, but could be coincidental. In fact, the vast majority of fatal cardiac events occur under resting conditions (such as sitting, driving, watching TV, sleeping, etc.) and not during physical activity!

Third, the majority of individuals who suffer a cardiac event during exercise have severe underlying heart disease to start with. In persons over 40, the most common underlying condition is coronary heart disease, that is, severe narrowing of the coronary arteries.

Finally, in many of these individuals, the cardiac event is preceded by cardiac symptoms (such as chest pain, severe breathlessness, and faintness), but for some reason these warning signs are either ignored or denied!

Based on these facts, it appears that exercise is indeed safe, provided that you take certain precautions. Furthermore, considering all the benefits exercise can bring, the real question is whether it is safe for you *not* to exercise!

12 When Eating Right Isn't Enough

You have now learned how to lower your cholesterol level by changing the kinds of foods you eat. In particular, you've learned how to cut down on dietary fat and cholesterol, how to increase your intake of complex carbohydrates and fiber, and how to lose weight and keep it off. If you have followed these guidelines, chances are you've reached your cholesterol goal and have accomplished it without a drastic change in your eating habits and lifestyle.

But perhaps you've had difficulty reaching your cholesterol goal. This does not mean that all you've learned so far was a waste of time. You probably were able to reduce your cholesterol to some degree, and this is a step in the right direction. Also, any additional treatment you may need will be built on the foundation of the new eating behavior you've just acquired.

Maybe It's Time to Get Some Help

There are several reasons why people cannot achieve their cholesterol goal by diet alone. Some people have a very high cholesterol level to start with, making it difficult for them to lower it to their goal, no matter how strict their diet is. Others have a defective genetic make-up, causing their body to resist any dietary changes. Still others have difficulty maintaining their new eating habits no matter how hard they try. In fact, it may take up to a year (or even longer) for them to get rid of their old unhealthy eating habits and learn new, healthy ones.

If you haven't reached your cholesterol goal after a few months on a sensible diet, it's probably time to get some help. Discuss the matter with your doctor. He or she will give you additional instructions, or may refer you to a registered dietitian. With the help of a dietitian, you will resume your diet under supervision, or you will be put on a stricter diet for a few months. Then, if despite all these efforts you are still unable to lower your cholesterol to the desired goal, your doctor may want to start you on medication.

The Role of the Doctor

If you have difficulty lowering your cholesterol on your own, your doctor can be of great assistance. He or she will review your medical history, focusing on risk factors that may increase the risk of heart disease (such as family history or cigarette smoking). Your doctor will then examine you and perform some basic tests, looking for additional clues for an increased risk (such as high blood pressure, blood vessel disease, or diabetes). Based on your cholesterol level and the above results, the doctor will prescribe a treatment plan that's right for you.

Your doctor or a staff member (a nurse, a nutritionist, or an assistant) will then review your past dietary history and ask questions about your current eating habits. He or she will explain the rationale for changing eating habits, guide you in selecting appropriate foods, and monitor your progress. Last, but not least, your doctor and the staff will provide you with the support and encouragement you need.

The Role of the Registered Dietitian

Registered dietitians (RDs) are educated in the science of nutrition and are professionally trained in dietary counseling and guidance. They must meet uniform standards for registration. The term "nutritionist" is often used, but you should know that these two terms do not necessarily have the same meaning—some nutritionists are registered dietitians, but others are not registered and may not have the training level of a registered dietitian.

The dietitian will first discuss with you the overall diet plan, with special emphasis on the connection between the kinds of foods you eat and your cholesterol level. The dietitian will then review with you food lists and tables, paying particular attention to foods that are rich in saturated fats, cholesterol, and calories. Depending on your particular needs, she may teach you how to keep daily food records, how to estimate food portion sizes, how to select foods at the supermarket, and how to prepare foods in the kitchen.

In addition, if the diet described in previous chapters has not lowered your cholesterol level enough, the dietitian may prescribe a stricter diet. This diet, termed the "Step-Two Diet" (see chart, below), differs from the "Step-One Diet" previously described in that the amount of saturated fats consumed is now limited to 7 percent of your total daily caloric intake, and the amount of dietary cholesterol is kept under 200 mg per day.

The preferable way for you to find a dietitian with expertise in cholesterol-lowering diets is to be referred by your doctor. This way, your doctor will be able to communicate with the dietitian on

"Step-One Diet"

Total fat	Less than 30% of total calories
Saturated fat	Less than 10% of total calories
Cholesterol	Less than 300 mg a day
Total calories	To achieve and maintain a desirable weight

"Step-Two Diet"

Total fat	Less than 30% of total calories
Saturated fat	Less than 7% of total calories
Cholesterol	Less than 200 mg a day
Total calories	To achieve and maintain a desirable weight

a regular basis, and provide you with a more individualized program. A listing of dietitians can also be obtained through state and district affiliates of the American Dietetic Association, through your local affiliate of the American Heart Association, and through local hospitals.

If you have a cholesterol problem and have been referred to a dietitian, it's important that you continue seeing the dietitian at regular intervals, at least until you have acquired new eating habits and feel you are in control of things. During that time, your doctor will measure your blood cholesterol level periodically. If you have attained your goal, long-term monitoring can begin. If not, your doctor may decide you need cholesterol-lowering medications to go along with your dietary changes.

Who Should Take Medications?

In most people, a cholesterol-lowering diet will be the only step needed to lower blood cholesterol to a desirable level. As we've seen, however, there are cases where diet alone is not enough. In such cases, medications may be included as part of the treatment. But even if your doctor does prescribe medications, you must continue your diet as before, since a proper diet will allow you to take less medication to reach your goal.

If your doctor decides you need a medication, the decision will be based on a number of factors, the most important ones being your blood cholesterol level, your response to the diet, and whether or not you have other risk factors for heart disease.

Patients whose cholesterol levels remain high despite being on a cholesterol-lowering diet should be considered for treatment. The National Cholesterol Education Program (NCEP) panel of experts has recommended that at least six months of diet and counseling be carried out before starting on medications. (There are exceptions to these rules, however. For patients who have an unusually high blood cholesterol, dietary treatment may be tried for less than six months. Likewise, in patients with definite coronary heart disease, in whom the urgency of lowering cholesterol is greater, it may be reasonable to consider medications sooner.)

As we've seen previously (in Chapter 3), LDL-cholesterol ("bad" cholesterol) levels are more precise than total cholesterol levels for predicting the risk of coronary heart disease, and are therefore preferred by doctors for making decisions about treatments to lower cholesterol.

Based on the NCEP guidelines, treatment with medications should be considered for any adult patient who, despite dietary treatment, has an LDL-cholesterol of 190 mg/dl or higher.

(Important: this is the LDL-cholesterol, *not* the total cholesterol. An LDL-cholesterol level of 190 mg/dl corresponds roughly to a total cholesterol of 280 mg/dl.)

If a patient has definite coronary heart disease (such as a history of angina or a heart attack) or two other risk factors (see checklist, page 15), his risk is increased, and medication could be given at a lower cholesterol level. Treatment in such patients should be considered at LDL-cholesterol levels of 160 mg/dl or higher (corresponding roughly to a total cholesterol of 240 mg/dl).

Remember:

• Diet is clearly the safest treatment available. Try your best to lower your blood cholesterol by dietary means first. Continue with your healthy eating habits even if medications are needed.

• Treatment with cholesterol-lowering medications is a long-term commitment, for years or even for life. Learn what the goals of the treatment are, and be aware of the side effects of medications.

• You are responsible, to a significant degree, for the success of your treatment. If problems arise, however, do not hesitate to get in touch with your doctor, nurse, dietitian, or pharmacist.

Cholesterol-Lowering Medications

It must be emphasized that treatment with cholesterol-lowering medications is a long-term commitment, for years or even for life. Diet is clearly the safest treatment available. You must try your best to lower your cholesterol by dietary means first, and continue with your new eating habits even if medications are needed.

Cholesterol-lowering medications work either by increasing the processing and removal of cholesterol from the body or by slowing its production in the liver. The medications most commonly used for lowering high blood cholesterol are the bile-acid binding resins (cholestyramine and colestipol), niacin, and lovastatin. Other medications, which are somewhat less effective for lowering cholesterol, are gemfibrozil and probucol.

Cholestyramine (Questran®)

Cholestyramine is a bile-acid binding resin, a substance that combines with bile acids in the intestine to form an insoluble substance which is then eliminated in the stools. (Bile acids are manufactured in the liver from cholesterol). By its action, cholestyramine increases the loss of bile acids and, as a result, the liver has to increase the use of cholesterol to manufacture new bile acids. As more cholesterol is being used by the liver, the level of cholesterol in the blood decreases.

How to use: Cholestyramine is a powder that must be mixed with water or fruit juice. It is available in 9-gram packets (each containing 4 grams of cholestyramine and 5 grams of orange flavored filler) and in 378-gram cans. The recommended dose is one packet or one scoopful, taken with meals, two to four times daily.

Cholestyramine powder should not be taken in its dry form. Always mix the powder with water or other fluids before ingesting. Place the contents of one packet or one level scoopful in a glass or cup. Add 2 to 6 ounces of water or fruit juice. Stir to uniform consistency. If you prefer, the powder can also be mixed with highly fluid soups or pulpy fruits with a high moisture content such as apple sauce or crushed pineapple.

Since cholestyramine may bind other drugs in the intestine and may interfere with their absorption, you should take other drugs at least one hour before or four hours after cholestyramine.

Side effects: The most common side effect is constipation. Less frequent side effects include bloating, stomach upset, nausea, and gas. Do not take cholestyramine if you have a history of severe constipation.

Colestipol (Colestid®)

Colestipol, another bile-acid binding resin, works in the same way as cholestyramine (see above).

How to use: Colestipol is a powder that must be mixed with water or fruit juice. It is available in 5-gram packets or in bottles containing 500 grams. Each packet or each level scoop supplies 5 grams of colestipol. The usual dose is one packet or one scoopful, taken with meals, two to four times daily.

Colestipol should always be mixed with water or other fluids before ingesting. It can be taken mixed in liquids such as water, fruit juice, milk, carbonated beverages, soup, or with pulpy fruits.

Since Colestipol may bind other drugs in the intestine and may interfere with their absorption, you should take other drugs at least one hour before or four hours after Colestipol.

Side effects: The most common side effect is constipation. Less frequent side effects include bloating, stomach upset, nausea, and gas. Do not take colestipol if you have a history of severe constipation.

Niacin (nicotinic acid)

Niacin acts on the liver, where it interferes with the manufacturing of some of the lipoproteins, including the LDLs (the major carriers of cholesterol). By its action, niacin decreases the amount of cholesterol in the blood. It lowers the triglycerides as well.

How to use: Niacin comes in tablets, in strengths of 100, 250, and 500 mg. Treatment is generally started at a low dose (for example 100 mg two or three times a day), then increased gradually every few days, until the maintenance dose is reached. The recommended maintenance dose is one or two 500 mg tablets, taken with or following meals, three times a day.

Niacin is also available in time-release capsules (such as Nicobid®). The capsule contains tiny niacin pellets designed to be slowly released in the bloodstream. There is virtually no flushing with these capsules. These preparations are more expensive.

Side effects: A common problem with niacin is flushing—a tingly, prickly sensation in the skin. The skin often turns pink or red, as though one were blushing or had been in the sun. The flush is strongest when first beginning to take niacin or when increasing the dosage level. After a few days of taking niacin at a given dose the flush tends to diminish and should not be of real concern. Taking an aspirin tablet either with the niacin or thirty minutes before will greatly decrease or even eliminate this problem. The use of time-release preparations will also reduce flushing.

Niacin can also cause abnormalities in laboratory tests. In particular, it can cause abnormal elevations of liver enzymes, uric acid (the substance that causes gout), and blood sugar. Other less common side effects include an itching rash and gastrointestinal symptoms. Niacin should not be taken by people with peptic ulcer, liver disease, diabetes, and gouty arthritis.

Important: Though at low dosages niacin is a vitamin, at the dosages taken to reduce cholesterol it is considered a drug! If you plan on taking niacin, consult your doctor first. The appropriate blood tests should be performed before beginning treatment and periodically thereafter.

Lovastatin (Mevacor®)

Lovastatin is the first of a new class of drugs that work by restraining the action of a key enzyme involved in the manufacturing of cholesterol in the liver. By its action, lovastatin slows down the production of cholesterol, resulting in the lowering of blood cholesterol levels.

How to use: Lovastatin comes in tablets of 20 mg. The recommended starting dose is 20 mg once a day taken with the evening meal. The usual maintenance dose is 20 to 80 mg a day in single or divided doses.

Side effects: Reported side effects include changes in bowel function, headaches, nausea, fatigue, sleeplessness, and skin rashes. A small number of patients may develop an elevation in levels of liver enzymes. Appropriate blood tests should be performed before beginning treatment and periodically thereafter.

There is also a concern that some patients may develop cataract (a condition in which the lens of the eye becomes cloudy). Although no effects have been detected to date in humans, this is still being investigated. An examination of the eye lens by an ophthalmologist (eye specialist) is therefore recommended, before treatment is begun and periodically thereafter.

Gemfibrozil (Lopid®)

Gemfibrozil is especially effective in lowering triglycerides, and it also reduces the level of LDL-cholesterol ("bad" cholesterol). There is also an associated increase in HDL-cholesterol ("good" cholesterol) level.

How to Use: Gemfibrozil is available as 300 mg capsules, and the usual dosage is two capsules twice daily, before the morning and evening meals.

Side effects: The most frequently reported side effects associated with gemfibrozil involve the gastrointestinal system. These include stomach upset, diarrhea, nausea, vomiting, and gas. Occasionally, it may cause abnormalities in laboratory tests, especially the blood count and liver function tests. It may also increase the formation of gallstones in susceptible people.

Probucol (Lorelco®)

Probucol slows down the production of cholesterol in the liver and increases its removal from the bloodstream. It therefore reduces the blood cholesterol level. The problem with probucol is that it also decreases the level of HDL-cholesterol ("good" cholesterol).

How to Use: Probucol is available in 250 mg tablets. The usual dose is two tablets twice daily, with the morning and evening meals.

Side effects: Probucol is generally well tolerated. Side effects may include diarrhea, abdominal pain, gas, and nausea.

Comparing the Medications

Cholesterol-lowering medications are not equally effective, and their side-effect profiles are different. As a basis of comparison, each medication can be viewed in terms of its ability to lower cholesterol levels, its long-term safety, and how convenient it is to use. Convenience of use relates to factors such as how the medication is used, how palatable it is, what its side effects are, and how much it costs.

The bile-acid binding resins (cholestyramine and colestipol) are moderately effective in lowering cholesterol (15-30% reduction in LDL-cholesterol levels). They are not absorbed into the body and are therefore safe for long-term use. Despite their efficacy and long-term safety, however, bile-acid binding resins are not always popular with patients. This is due to the gritty texture of the powder, the inconvenience of carrying and consuming a packet of powder away from home, and troublesome side effects such as bloating and constipation. The best buys among resins are the cans of powder. You pay extra for the convenience of individual packets.

Niacin is as effective as the resins in lowering cholesterol levels (15 -30% reduction). It has been used as a cholesterol-lowering agent for many years, and its long-term safety is established. Niacin comes in a convenient tablet form and is inexpensive (in its generic form). The major problem with niacin is the frequent side effects, especially the flushing, itching rash, and gastrointestinal symptoms. These side effects are usually lessened by reducing the dose or by using time-release preparations. These preparations are more expensive than the generic form of niacin.

Lovastatin is the most effective cholesterol-lowering agent available today (25-45% reduction). It comes in a convenient tablet

	Cholesterol Lowering (%)	Long-term Safety	Convenience of Use	Side Effects
Cholestyramine (Questran®)	15-30%	Yes	Powder Gritty texture	Constipation, bloating, nausea, gas
Colestipol (Colestid®)	15-30%	Yes	Powder Gritty texture	Constipation, bloating, nausea, gas
Niacin (nicotinic acid)	15-30%	Yes	Tablets Easy to take	Flushing, itchy rash, stomach upset
Lovastatin (Mevacor®)	25-45%	Not established	Tablets Easy to take	Stomach upset, headache, nausea, fatigue, skin rash
Gemfibrozil (Lopid®)	5-15%	Yes	Tablets Easy to take	Stomach upset, diarrhea, nausea, gas
Probucol (Lorelco®)	10-15%	Not established	Tablets Easy to take	Stomach upset, diarrhea, nausea, gas

Chart 9. Summary of the characteristics of commonly used cholesterol-lowering medications

form and is easy to use. It is well tolerated by most patients and has fewer side effects than the resins and niacin. Since lovastatin has been in use for only a few years, its long-term safety is not yet established. Once its safety can be established, however, doctors will probably turn more frequently to the use of lovastatin for treating high blood cholesterol.

Gemfibrozil is not as effective as lovastatin, niacin, and the resins for lowering cholesterol (only 5-15% reduction). It is quite effective for lowering high triglyceride levels, however. It also raises the HDL-cholesterol ("good" cholesterol). The long-term safety of gemfibrozil has recently been established in a large-scale clinical trial. Gemfibrozil comes in tablet form and is easy to take. It is generally well tolerated, although it sometimes causes gastrointestinal symptoms.

Probucol reduces cholesterol levels, but to a lesser degree than do lovastatin, niacin, and the resins (10-15% reduction). The problem with probucol is that it also lowers the level of HDL-cholesterol ("good" cholesterol), and may (at least theoretically) increase the risk of heart disease. It appears to be safe, but its long-term safety has not yet been proven in large-scale trials. Probucol is generally well tolerated, although it may cause gastrointestinal symptoms in some patients.

13 Other Factors That Increase Your Risk

We've seen the effect high blood cholesterol can have on the build-up of fatty plaques within the walls of the arteries. We've also learned how we can reduce our chances of developing heart disease by lowering blood cholesterol through changes in the diet. But this may not be enough, since elevated blood cholesterol is not the only factor increasing the risk of heart disease.

Other conditions and habits, such as cigarette smoking and high blood pressure, also increase your risk. If you smoke, for example, you are more likely to suffer a heart attack, and you'll do so at a younger age. It wouldn't make any sense if you worked so hard to lower your cholesterol while, at the same time, continued smoking or ignored your high blood pressure.

Some risk factors are not under our control. These include age, gender, and heredity. Among the risk factors we can control, three are considered major: high blood cholesterol, cigarette smoking, and high blood pressure. Other risk factors include: diabetes, obesity, lack of exercise, and stress.

Risk Factors Not under Our Control

There are a number of risk factors that are beyond our ability to control. For example, if you are a male or if there is history of heart disease in your family, there is nothing you can do about it. But don't be discouraged. You can still reduce your risk of heart disease by making some simple changes in your lifestyle, such as eating the right foods, quitting smoking, and exercising regularly.

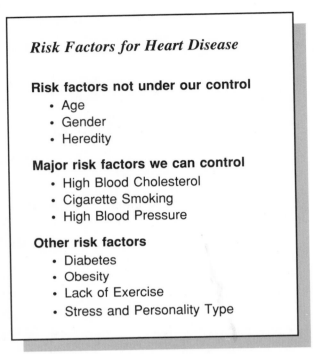

Risk Factors for Heart Disease

Risk factors not under our control
- Age
- Gender
- Heredity

Major risk factors we can control
- High Blood Cholesterol
- Cigarette Smoking
- High Blood Pressure

Other risk factors
- Diabetes
- Obesity
- Lack of Exercise
- Stress and Personality Type

Age

Although heart disease is not caused by aging itself, it is more common among older people. In general, the longer a person lives, the greater his chances of having a heart attack. It has been shown that atherosclerosis begins at an early age, then progresses slowly over the years, often without any symptoms. It becomes a major cause of illness and death for people in their fifties and sixties.

Gender

Men have a higher incidence of heart disease than women in the same age range. The fact that women are less likely to develop heart disease is due to the presence of natural female sex hormones which appear to protect against the build-up of plaques within the arteries. Following menopause, women "catch up" with men, and by the age of sixty they develop the disease at a similar rate.

Heredity

Generally, if a person's parent, brother, or sister have had a heart attack at a relatively young age (in their forties and fifties), that person is at greater risk of developing heart disease. In addition to this inherited influence, the home environment may also play a role. Studies have shown, for example, that when both parents smoke, their children are more likely to become smokers and therefore have a higher risk of heart disease.

Major Risk Factors We Can Control

High blood cholesterol is one of the three major risk factors. The two others are cigarette smoking and high blood pressure. These risk factors are controllable, which means we can do something about them.

High Blood Cholesterol

As we've seen, high blood cholesterol is an important risk factor for heart disease. The higher your cholesterol level, the greater your risk of having a heart attack. You can lower your blood cholesterol by changing your diet—cutting down on saturated fat and cholesterol, and eating foods rich in complex carbohydrates and fiber.

Cigarette Smoking

The evidence linking cigarette smoking to coronary heart disease is overwhelming. People who smoke a pack of cigarettes a day, for example, have more than twice the risk of having a heart attack than nonsmokers. In general, the risk is directly proportional to the number of cigarettes smoked. (For more on smoking, see Chapter 14).

People who quit smoking have a lesser risk of heart disease than those who continue to smoke. In fact, once the habit is given up, the risk gradually declines toward the same level as that of people who have never smoked. Within two years after quitting, the risk of a heart attack in former smokers is about half that of smokers. After ten years the risk is lowered to practically the same level as those who have never smoked.

High Blood Pressure

A chronic elevation of the blood pressure leads to increased deposit of fatty plaques in the walls of the arteries. This process is especially common in the major arteries that conduct blood to vital organs, such as the heart and brain. The higher your blood pressure, the higher your risk of developing a heart attack or a stroke. You can reduce your risk by getting your blood pressure under control. (For more on high blood pressure, see Chapter 15).

Other Risk Factors

Diabetes

Diabetes mellitus (or "sugar diabetes") is a condition in which the blood sugar level is abnormally high. Diabetes may be caused either by insufficient insulin or by the body's inability to effectively use the insulin it produces. (Insulin is a hormone produced by the pancreas and used by the body to break down sugar and other carbohydrates.) When too little insulin is produced, sugar accumulates in the blood.

Patients with diabetes have a much higher risk of developing atherosclerosis than nondiabetics. Therefore, diabetics have an increased frequency of heart attacks, strokes, and peripheral vascular disease (poor circulation to the legs). Those who develop diabetes at an early age are at greater risk than those in whom the disease occurs in later years.

Obesity

Studies have shown that the risk of developing heart disease is greater in obese persons. Excess weight may not directly affect the heart itself, but it certainly does aggravate several other risk factors. Indeed, obesity increases a person's chance of developing high blood cholesterol, high blood pressure, and diabetes. (For more on obesity and weight loss, see Chapter 10).

Lack of Exercise

The role of exercise in the prevention of heart disease has become a subject of increasing interest. Several studies have shown a statistical link between a sedentary lifestyle and increased incidence of heart disease. Other investigations have shown, although not conclusively, that an exercise training program may decrease the chances of getting a heart attack.

Regular exercise can also help reduce several risk factors, such as high blood pressure, high blood cholesterol, and obesity. With exercise, there is often a reduction in the level of triglycerides and cholesterol in the blood, as well as an elevation of the HDL (the "good" cholesterol). Along with a proper diet, exercise is helpful in burning excess calories and reducing body weight. Finally, many smokers give up their habit after they start exercising, particularly when they choose an exercise they enjoy. (For more on exercise, see Chapter 11).

Stress and Personality Type

In general terms, stress occurs when there is an imbalance between excessive environmental demands and the person's ability to cope with them. If recurrent or prolonged, stress may harm the person's health and well-being. Not all stress, however, is necessarily bad. All of us need a certain amount of stress to add variety and spice to life, to push us to achieve goals. Some people even thrive on stress—they find working under pressure or against deadlines highly stimulating.

A good deal has been written about the possible role of personality type in causing heart disease. Much of this stems from the research of two San Francisco physicians, Drs. Friedman and Rosenman. After interviewing a large number of heart attack patients, they began to see a common behavior pattern in many of these patients, which they termed "Type A behavior." They concluded that a person with a hard-driven and time-conscious personality (Type A) is at a higher risk of developing a heart attack than a person who is calm and easy going (Type B).

Typically, a Type A person is competitive, shows a sense of urgency about time, and has an unrelenting determination to forge

Helpful Tips

Reducing Stress in Your Life

• Be realistic and set practical goals. People who expect too much of themselves can experience an increase in tension if things don't work out.

• Identify the activities you find satisfying in and of themselves, and focus on enjoying them, rather than on your performance or what rewards the activities might bring.

• Organize your time. Identify the time wasters. Leave yourself more time than you think you'll need to get somewhere or to accomplish something.

• Set priorities. Divide your tasks into three categories— essential, important, and trivial—and forget about the trivial.

• Get regular exercise. Exercise will increase your stamina, recharge your energy, and get rid of excess tension.

• Be sure to get enough sleep and rest because fatigue can reduce your ability to cope with stress. Eat regular, balanced meals with enough variety to assure good nutrition.

• Listen to your body—it will let you know when you are pushing too hard. When you get tired, slow down and take time to enjoy the world around you.

• Don't waste your anger on trivial matters—which you can do nothing about anyway—such as a delayed train, a traffic tie up, or a person who is rude to you.

• Learn good working habits. Clear your desk of all papers except those relating to the immediate problem at hand. Do things in the order of their importance.

• Learn relaxation techniques (such as muscle relaxation, deep breathing exercises, meditation, yoga, or biofeedback). Some of these techniques will require professional help to learn.

Continued

• On a tightly-scheduled day, take a few minutes between appointments or activities for a relaxation break, such as stretching, breathing, or a short walk.

• Avoid the use of tranquilizers, sleeping pills, alcohol, or tobacco. These addictive substances may provide temporary relief from stress, but will not cure the underlying cause of the problem.

• Talk it out. Problems often seem much worse when you carry them all alone. Talking to a trusted friend or relative can help you sort things out and unload some of the burden.

• Finally, if stress and its effects do get out of hand, it's time to seek professional counseling or therapy. Professionals in a position to help you include the family doctor, nurses, social workers, clergy, psychologists, and psychiatrists.

ahead quickly, both socially and economically. In other words, this is a person who wants to do too many things in too little time. The Type A person is often a "workaholic" who takes little, if any, time to relax for fear of falling behind. He may be quick-tempered, compulsive, suspicious, and even hostile. In contrast, the Type B person is more relaxed, less competitive, and not so driven by time and the need to succeed.

The possible association between personality type and the risk of heart disease is still the subject of continuing controversy. A few studies have found that Type A men had twice the risk of developing heart disease as did Type B men. More recent large-scale studies, however, have not confirmed those findings.

Regardless of the roots of Type A behavior, an important question is whether or not we should try to modify it. In our success-oriented, competitive society, the Type A person is rewarded by achieving many of the goals that we hold in such high esteem, such as money, status, and power. Also, most Type A persons seem to enjoy their hectic, fast-paced lives and have no desire to change. They prefer to think of themselves as competent and competitive rather than "compulsive" and "hostile," as conscientious and productive rather than "time-slaves" and "workaholics."

Reducing the Risk—It's in Your Hands!

The fact that some risk factors can be changed should be regarded as good news. By making changes in your own lifestyle (eating a proper diet, quitting smoking, and exercising on a regular basis), you can modify or even eliminate these risk factors, and therefore be in a position to prevent, or at least delay, the progression of atherosclerosis and heart disease.

Several risk factors (such as high blood pressure, high cholesterol level, and diabetes) do not cause any symptoms during their early stages; they are "silent." For this reason, you should have regular screenings for these conditions—have your blood pressure, blood cholesterol, and blood sugar checked periodically.

Generally, the initial checkup should begin at age 20 and be repeated at least every five years. In addition, a blood pressure reading should be obtained every year or two, because blood pressure can creep up unexpectedly. Older people may need a medical checkup at more frequent intervals. Checkups are particularly important if there is a family history of heart disease, high blood pressure, high cholesterol level, or diabetes.

You may regard these preventive measures as a personal investment that can only have a positive return. It's true, there is no guarantee that modifying your risk factors will prevent heart disease in all cases. There is no doubt, however, that if you take these positive steps, you will have better general health, you will be in better physical shape, and you will feel better about yourself. And, as a bonus, you will probably live longer as well.

14 Giving Up the Smoking Habit

"Warning: The Surgeon General Has Determined That Cigarette Smoking is Dangerous to Your Health." A similar warning label now appears on every pack of cigarettes. Since the Surgeon General's landmark report in 1964, the percentage of smokers in the population has been declining steadily. While this is encouraging, there are still over 50 million Americans who smoke cigarettes today, comprising approximately 30 percent of adult males and 25 percent of adult females.

The Hazards of Smoking

Cigarette smoking is one of the major public health hazards in this country, resulting in over 300,000 tobacco-related deaths each year. Smokers can expect a shorter life span than nonsmokers. For example, the life expectancy of a 25-year-old who smokes two packs a day is about 8 years shorter than that of a nonsmoker.

Smoking is one of the three major risk factors for heart disease (the other two are high cholesterol and high blood pressure). People who smoke one pack of cigarettes a day have more than twice the risk of having a heart attack than do non-smokers.

Smoking is also the leading cause of chronic lung disease (chronic bronchitis and emphysema), the number one cause of lung cancer, and a major cause of mouth and throat cancer. Most smokers show a progressive decline of respiratory function and a reduction of exercise tolerance, even before signs of disease appear.

A pregnant woman who smokes has an increased risk of miscarriage, stillbirth, and of having a low birth weight infant. In addition, smoking during pregnancy may result in retarded physical and mental development of the child. Quitting smoking can greatly improve pregnancy outcome.

How Smoking Affects Your Body

Smoking is associated with a certain degree of addiction to nicotine, a powerful drug found in tobacco. As smoke is inhaled, nicotine passes through the membrane of the lung tissue and rapidly enters the bloodstream. Then, within ten seconds, the inhaled nicotine reaches the brain, where it induces the release of adrenaline-like substances, called catecholamines. The effect of these substances is to accelerate the heart rate and raise the blood pressure. These changes in the body's metabolism are the "lift" that some smokers crave.

Addicted smokers must keep a continuous amount of nicotine circulating in the blood and going to the brain. If that amount falls below a certain level, or if they stop smoking, they may experience unpleasant withdrawal symptoms. Symptoms of withdrawal may include the following: headache, nausea, fatigue, drowsiness, difficulty falling asleep, inability to concentrate, irritability, anxiety, depression, and a craving for tobacco. If you are a smoker and try to quit, be prepared to accept withdrawal symptoms as a natural consequence of stopping. Withdrawal is a temporary condition that, though often unpleasant, is not harmful.

In addition to nicotine, cigarette smoke contains harmful gases, the most dangerous one being carbon monoxide, a colorless and odorless gas. Carbon monoxide has a stronger attraction (by 200 times!) for red blood cells than does oxygen. Since red blood cells are meant to carry oxygen throughout the body, this means that carbon monoxide is replacing oxygen, therefore interfering with the distribution of oxygen to the body cells.

Carbon monoxide seems to be nicotine's accomplice in many assaults on the smoker's body. Studies have shown that carbon

SURGEON GENERAL'S WARNING: Smoking Causes
Heart Disease, Lung Cancer, and Emphysema

monoxide makes it easier for fatty substances to pass through the
walls of arteries. This may be one of the mechanisms leading to the
build-up of fatty plaques within the arteries. The adrenaline released
by jolts of inhaled nicotine aids this process by affecting fat cells all
over the body, causing them to pour fatty acids into the bloodstream.
Every time a person smokes, the blood level of these fatty acids
increases.

Elevated levels of fatty acids also have a harmful effect on the
blood clotting process. Studies have shown that the platelets (tiny
corpuscles that participate in clotting) become stickier in smokers.
This may explain why smokers get more heart attacks than nonsmokers: their blood more readily forms clots, which may block a
coronary artery, thereby causing a heart attack.

Cigarette smoking also lowers the blood level of HDL, the
"good" cholesterol. As we have already seen (in Chapter 3), HDL
has a protective effect against the build-up of fatty plaques in the
arteries. By lowering HDL levels, smoking may increase the risk of
heart disease. If you smoke, one of the steps you should take to raise
your HDL level is to quit smoking.

In addition to nicotine and harmful gases, cigarette smoke also
contains tars—solid chemical particles which, when inhaled, con-
dense as sticky substances in the lungs. These tars interfere with the
normal function of the lungs and may result in lung disease. Indeed,
smoking is the leading cause of emphysema, an irreversible condition which reduces the lung's elasticity and destroys its tiny air sacs.
Chemicals present in tar are known to produce cancer. Cancers
begin when tars produce abnormal cells in the mouth, throat, and
lungs; these irregular cells then develop into tumors.

The damage done by cigarettes is "dose related," meaning that
each cigarette does some harm. Each additional inhalation then
increases the damage. There is no such thing as a safe level of

smoking, nor such a thing as a safe cigarette. Research has shown that cutting down on the number of cigarettes smoked, as well as smoking those which have efficient filters and less tar and nicotine, may reduce the risk of serious illness. However, if you smoke and really want to avoid the dangers of smoking, just cutting down is not the best way to go. The only certain way (and generally the easiest way) to protect your health is to quit smoking altogether.

Smokers themselves are not the only ones affected by tobacco smoke. Although the evidence so far is not as conclusive as it is for smokers, nonsmokers exposed to tobacco (for example, nonsmokers married to smokers) may also be at risk. Several studies have shown a relationship between so-called "passive (or involuntary) smoking" and the incidence of lung cancer.

SURGEON GENERAL'S WARNING: Quitting Smoking Now Greatly Reduces Serious Risks to Your Health

As you can see, cigarette smoking is a health hazard of the first order. The good news, however, is that you can still reverse many of the adverse effects of smoking by quitting now. Studies have shown that ex-smokers have a lower risk of developing heart disease than those who continue to smoke. Once the habit is given up, the risk gradually declines over the years. Within two years after quitting, the risk of a heart attack in former smokers is about half the risk in smokers. After ten years, the risk is practically the same as for nonsmokers!

Why You Smoke—and Some Healthier Alternatives

Most smokers begin to smoke in their teenage years. Peer pressure may be necessary for those first cigarettes, since the sensations are mostly unpleasant in the beginning. Smoking then becomes a learned behavior. If you are ready to quit smoking, you must first become aware of your habits and identify the reasons behind them. Then, you must make a conscious effort to replace these old habits with new, healthier ones.

Perhaps you smoke for the stimulant effect—it gives you a "lift" or appears to get you going. You are likely to begin the day with a cigarette. You may want to smoke more when you feel tired, and get a "kick" out of smoking. Instead of a cigarette, take a brisk walk, do a few stretches at your desk, or just open the window and breathe fresh air.

You may smoke to occupy your hands, or for the pleasure of handling the paraphernalia of cigarettes. You probably have certain rituals about smoking: your favorite brand, the way you take out the cigarette, and the way you light it up with matches or a lighter. You enjoy watching the smoke, perhaps blowing smoke rings, or exhaling through the nose. Instead of a cigarette, try substituting other objects to keep your hands busy, such as a pen or a pencil, a coin, worry beads, or some other harmless object.

Maybe you smoke to relax, as a reward for getting a job done, or to enhance the pleasure of eating, driving a car, or having a conversation. Chances are you most enjoy smoking after a meal, a cocktail, or a cup of coffee. It will make it easier for you to quit if you'll recall what cigarettes can do to your health. Is it really worth it? Instead of smoking, get involved in social activities or start on an exercise program, and you'll probably find you don't really miss your cigarettes.

You may smoke to ease "stress," when you are anxious, angry, or upset. For you, a cigarette is like a tranquilizer. If you've been using smoking as a coping mechanism, you will soon realize that cigarettes will not resolve your problems. Instead, find activities that will help you through these difficult moments. Again, social activities and exercise can be very useful substitutes for cigarettes in times of stress.

Perhaps you reach for a cigarette merely out of habit—for you, smoking has become an unconscious act. You light up or finish a smoke without being aware of it or taking much pleasure in it. You may not even enjoy smoking, but you keep buying and burning packs of cigarettes because you don't really know what to do without them. You will not find it hard to quit once you make an effort to be conscious of each cigarette you smoke, and the conditions under which you smoke.

Finally, for some, smoking has become an addiction, a continual act of craving. You have become a chain smoker—your craving begins as soon as one cigarette is stubbed out. You wake up in the morning and, despite a hacking cough, you reach for a cigarette. For you, quitting is undoubtedly hard and must be generally done "cold turkey," since cutting down gradually is almost impossible. You'll have to quit smoking as a conscious act of will, replacing your addiction with a turn toward health and self-control.

Kicking the Habit

If you smoke and want to quit, you can take heart in the fact that each year more than 3 million people quit smoking for good. Although smoking cessation programs of one kind or another are helpful for some, most people who stop do so on their own. Motivation appears to be the key element in many of the success stories. No one method of quitting works for everyone: some stop "cold turkey," while others cut down gradually. Many smokers are helped by joining low-cost smoking cessation clinics.

With a self-help program, smokers are provided with brochures, books, audio tapes, and kits that will lead them through a program of smoking cessation on their own. A variety of voluntary organizations (such as the American Lung Association, the American Heart Association, and the American Cancer Society) offer helpful literature and various materials for smokers who want to break the habit.

A number of organizations, public and private, hold low-cost smoking cessation clinics that treat smoking in a group format. Programs consist of a series of meetings. Usually included are lectures, inspirational messages, films, and group interaction. Other methods for smoking cessation include individual and group counseling, hypnosis, and behavior modification.

Helpful Tips

Quitting Smoking

• List your reasons for quitting. Concentrate on the reasons that are personally very important to you. Whenever you are tempted to smoke again, use the list to remind you about the unacceptable and unappetizing aspects of smoking.

• If the long-term health benefits of quitting aren't sufficient motivation because they are too abstract or removed, concentrate on the immediate rewards of not smoking, such as cleaner breath, fresher clothes and hair, and improved stamina.

• Study your smoking habit. Keep a smoking diary to determine when and under what circumstances you smoke. The act of recording will help you become more conscious of your smoking.

• Plan when you'll quit. Set a date several weeks in advance and plan ahead. Some people are helped by tapering off smoking before the actual target date. Talk to friends who have quit and learn what to expect.

• Let other people know you are quitting. This will help to initiate social support, and put social pressure on you to succeed. When someone offers you a cigarette, decline politely but firmly. Don't be afraid to ask others not to smoke in your presence.

• A relapse does not necessarily spell the end of your efforts to quit. In fact, most smokers succeed only after having made several attempts to quit.

• Watch your weight. Eat small snacks more frequently (5 or 6 times a day), rather than 3 heavy meals. Keep a supply of low-calorie snacks on hand while reading or watching television. Avoid rich desserts, and eat fruits instead.

• The early period of quitting is not a good time for a stringent diet—this may only lead to a return to the smoking habit.

Continued

• If you miss holding a cigarette, use substitutes such as a pen or pencil, a paper clip, or a key chain. If you miss the oral stimulation of a cigarette, use oral substitutes such as tooth-picks, sugarless gum or candy, or a plastic straw.

• Increase your exercise. Regular exercise will help minimize the weight gain, will provide a sense of physical well-being, and will relieve "jittery nerves" and tension.

• Identify times when you are most likely to smoke, and plan other activities, such as taking a walk after dinner instead of having a second cup of coffee and a cigarette.

• Reward yourself! Put away "cigarette money" to save for a trip, records or CDs, or new clothes. Or use the money periodically to buy a little something you wouldn't normally purchase, like a book, magazine, or fresh flowers.

The most effective strategy is to choose a specific date in the future, and when that date arrives, quit smoking "cold turkey." The first few days are the most difficult, when the various withdrawal symptoms may occur. After that, the physical and psychological needs gradually begin to lessen.

Another strategy, somewhat less effective, is the step-by-step method. Some may use progressively stronger filters or switch to cigarette brands of lower tar and nicotine content. Others may adopt such measures as delaying lighting up, inhaling smoke fewer times, laying down the cigarette between puffs, or extinguishing the ciga-rette after smoking it for only a short time.

Since smoking depresses the appetite by dulling the senses of taste and smell, one of the immediate advantages of not smoking is being able to truly taste and smell food again. Because ex-smokers may satisfy their oral craving with food, and due to some other metabolic changes, many people gain weight when they quit. You can prevent or at least minimize weight gain by avoiding high-calorie foods and by starting a moderate exercise program. Even if you gain pounds, you'll be able to return to your normal weight once you get used to your new and healthier lifestyle.

The rewards from giving up smoking can be considerable. Soon, you'll feel an increased sense of well-being. There will be a gradual improvement in your stamina, and a slow disappearance of your hacking cough. The socially undesirable features of cigarette smoking you've become subject to (such as bad breath, stained teeth and fingers, and cigarette odor in clothes) will fade away rapidly. And, last but not least, your potential risk of developing heart and lung disease will decline steadily, and you will be able to live a longer and healthier life.

15 Getting Your Blood Pressure Under Control

High blood pressure (or hypertension) affects about one out of every six adult Americans, making it one of the most common medical problems in this country. In most patients, the elevated blood pressure produces no symptoms—it is "silent." If not treated, however, it can lead to progressive damage to blood vessels and to other vital organs (especially the heart, brain, and kidneys). As a matter of fact, hypertensive people are five times more likely to have a heart attack than people whose blood pressure is normal. For these reasons, hypertension has been referred to as the "silent killer."

If your blood pressure is elevated, there are several steps you can take to bring it under control. You can cut down on salt, lose weight (if overweight), exercise regularly, and learn to relax. Even if these steps do not bring your blood pressure all the way back to normal, they will often bring it down to a safer level. Besides, these changes in lifestyle will surely benefit your general health and well-being, and they may prolong your life.

Your Blood Pressure

Blood pressure is the force of blood against the walls of the arteries, created by the heart as it pumps blood to all parts of the body. When blood pressure is measured, two pressures are recorded in numbers. The higher number, called the systolic pressure, is generated when the heart contracts and ejects blood under pressure into the arteries. The lower number, called the diastolic pressure, is produced when the heart relaxes between beats, as the pressure within the arteries gradually falls.

Blood pressure levels vary widely among individuals. In a given person there is, in addition, variation of blood pressure readings throughout the day. In fact, readings taken just minutes apart may be 10 to 20 "points" different from one another. Some of these differences may be due to excitement, nervousness, or physical activity. During exercise and emotional stress, blood pressure tends to rise. During resting periods and sleep, on the other hand, it tends to come down.

Blood pressure is measured using a blood pressure machine and a stethoscope. It is expressed in millimeters of mercury (mmHg). For example, if the systolic pressure is 120 mmHg and the diastolic pressure is 80 mmHg, the result is a blood pressure of 120/80 mmHg, expressed as "one-twenty over eighty."

High blood pressure is an excessive amount of pressure within the arteries. While there is no clear definition of where "normal"

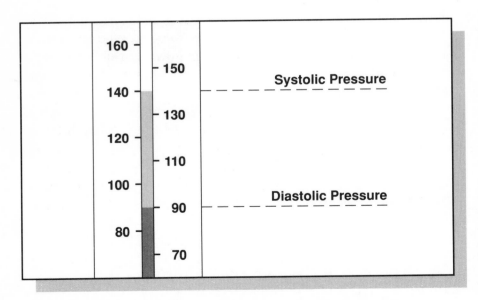

Chart 10. Blood pressure readings of 140/90 are generally considered to be at the upper limit of normal.

ends and "abnormal" begins, most physicians use pressure readings of 140/90 as the upper limit of normal. Readings between 140/90 and 160/95 are generally considered "borderline," and readings over 160/95 are considered "high." The higher the blood pressure, the higher the risk of having a heart attack or a stroke.

What Causes High Blood Pressure?

In a small number of patients with hypertension, a specific cause can be identified—this is called "secondary" hypertension. Nearly all the secondary forms are related to either an abnormality in kidney function or an excessive secretion of certain hormones. More commonly, however, a specific cause cannot be found, and the condition is termed "essential" (or "primary") hypertension. Although the cause is unknown, several factors have been implicated in the development of essential hypertension, including heredity, salt intake, obesity, and stress.

Heredity. It appears that a tendency to develop high blood pressure is passed from parent to child. A person who had one or two hypertensive parents, for example, has a greater chance of developing high blood pressure than a person who did not have hypertensive parents.

Salt intake. People living in modern industrialized countries tend to consume too much salt (often 10 to 20 times the amount needed by the body!). Studies have shown that hypertension tends to increase with higher levels of salt intake. It is therefore likely that high salt intake is responsible, at least to some degree, for many cases of hypertension. Salt restriction will lower the blood pressure in most hypertensive patients.

Obesity. High blood pressure is more common among obese individuals. Obese children and adults have an increased likelihood of developing hypertension compared to people of normal weight. Weight loss in obese people is often helpful in controlling an elevated blood pressure level.

Stress. In some people, emotional stress may worsen their hypertension. Utilizing relaxation techniques can reduce blood pressure, at least temporarily, in many hypertensive persons. Decreasing the level of stress or finding positive ways of dealing with stress may help lower the blood pressure in those individuals.

What High Blood Pressure Can Do to Your Body

Most patients with hypertension have no symptoms relating to their blood pressure! Hypertension is generally diagnosed when blood pressure is measured during the course of a routine physical examination. When symptoms do occur, they are usually vague. Some patients may develop recurrent headaches (typically upon awakening in the morning), become fatigued easily, or complain of dizziness, blurry vision, or nose bleeds.

If high blood pressure is allowed to remain out of control for too long, it can lead to deposits of fatty plaques in the walls of the arteries (atherosclerosis). This process is especially common in the aorta (the body's main artery) and in the major arterial branches conducting blood to vital organs, especially the heart, brain, and kidneys. It eventually results in damage to one or more of these vital organs, termed "target organs."

Effects on the Heart. As we've seen, high blood pressure is a major risk factor for coronary heart disease, that is, the build-up of fatty plaques inside the coronary arteries. Total blockage of a coronary artery may in turn result in damage to an area of the heart muscle (heart attack). The heart may also suffer from the constant strain of having to pump blood against higher resistance, and it may weaken to the point of causing heart failure.

Effects on the Brain. Hypertension is a major risk factor for the development of strokes. A stroke results from the total blockage of blood flow in one of the arteries conducting blood to the brain. Other times, it may result from the rupture (bursting) of a blood vessel, followed by a hemorrhage (bleeding) into the brain tissue. In either case, the damaged brain tissue cannot function properly, and

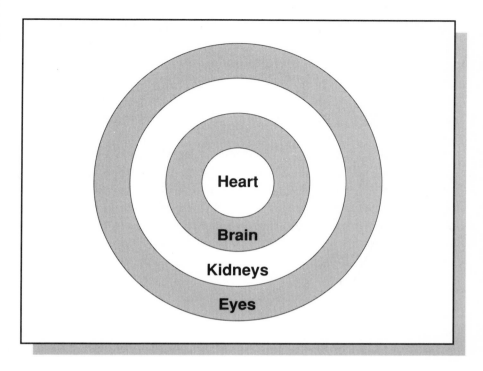

Chart 11. Long-standing hypertension may result in damage to one or more vital organs, termed "target organs."

manifestations of a stroke (such as weakness of a limb, paralysis, or loss of speech) develop.

Effects on the Kidneys. Being rich in blood vessels, the kidneys are particularly susceptible to the damaging effects of hypertension. The long-standing elevation of the blood pressure leads to a progressive narrowing of the small arteries within the kidneys. As a result, the kidneys are unable to function properly, and waste products accumulate in the bloodstream, eventually leading to kidney failure.

Effects on the Eyes. The layered lining of the eye (retina), containing the light-sensitive receptors, is rich in tiny blood vessels. Long-standing hypertension can cause serious eye problems, such as bleeding (retinal hemorrhages) or the formation of blood clots in the tiny blood vessels. Depending on the exact location of the problem in the eye, these complications can cause no symptoms or they can cause reduced vision and blindness.

What You Can Do about Your Blood Pressure

The main reason for controlling hypertension is to prevent its potential complications. Even in its mild form, hypertension is a progressive disease that leads to a significant increase in the risk of having a heart attack or a stroke. Studies have shown that long-standing untreated hypertension is associated with a shortening of life by 10 years or more. But even people with severe hypertension can have a significant reduction in their risk if they are started on a treatment program.

Whether or not you have to take medications to lower your blood pressure, you will surely benefit from making some changes in your lifestyle. If your blood pressure elevation is mild, these measures may be sufficient to bring your blood pressure down to a safe level. Other times, these steps will be only partially effective, but will surely benefit your general health.

As we've seen, high salt intake is responsible, at least in part, for many cases of hypertension. *Cutting down on salt* is therefore advisable in most hypertensive patients. You can accomplish the desired degree of salt restriction by following several simple guidelines: (a) do not add salt to food during cooking or at the table, (b) avoid obviously salty foods such as pickles, sauerkraut, and salted peanuts, (c) avoid or minimize the use of canned or prepacked foods to which too much salt has been added, and (d) recognize the salt (sodium) content of various foods, antacids, and drugs, by reading the label. (See below, Cutting Down On Salt).

In obese people, *weight loss* is an effective way of reducing the blood pressure. In general, the more weight is lost, the lower the blood pressure will be. If you are overweight and have discovered that you also have high blood pressure, this should be a strong motivation for you to lose weight. As we've already seen (in Chapter 10), the biggest problem with weight control is not

Helpful Tips

Controlling Your Blood Pressure

• Even if you take medications to lower your blood pressure, it's important that you make positive changes in your lifestyle: cut down on salt; lose extra weight; exercise regularly; quit smoking; and learn to relax.

• If you have hypertension, have your blood pressure checked every few weeks, even after you have achieved good control. Don't be concerned if the pressure fluctuates somewhat between visits—it may reflect nothing more than temporary stress or a normal variation.

• The use of blood pressure medications can cause some side effects. These are generally mild and temporary. If you feel you are experiencing a side effect, don't just stop treatment. Call your doctor and discuss the matter with him.

• Take your medications as directed. Try taking them routinely at the same time of the day, so you won't forget. If you happen to miss a dose or two, don't take all the doses you have missed at one time to make up for the loss. Just get back on the prescribed schedule.

• High blood pressure is a chronic disease. Therefore, treatment will almost certainly be lifelong. Keep taking your medications even if you feel perfectly well.

• It may take some time and effort to achieve the treatment goals. The reward for your efforts is the knowledge that effective control of high blood pressure will eventually lead to a healthier and longer life.

necessarily how to lose a few pounds, but rather how to keep those extra pounds off for extended periods of time. Therefore, if you want to succeed in losing weight and keeping it off, you must first change your eating habits.

Regular exercise helps lower blood pressure by burning up excess calories and helping in weight loss. The recommended type of exercise is "aerobic", such as walking, jogging, and swimming. (For more on exercise, see Chapter 11). During aerobic exercise, the systolic pressure usually goes up but the diastolic pressure stays at the same level or may go down. To obtain a full conditioning effect, you should exercise at a moderate level, for at least 20 to 30 minutes, 3 or 4 times a week.

Relieving stress through *relaxation* will reduce blood pressure, at least temporarily, in many hypertensive individuals. You can reduce your exposure to stress by working fewer hours or taking more vacation time. Various types of relaxation techniques (such as meditation and biofeedback) have also been used with some success to improve ways of dealing with stress.

If you smoke, you should *quit smoking*. Although cigarette smoking has little direct effect on the blood pressure itself, it is another major risk factor for the development of heart disease.

If your blood pressure is too high, your doctor may decide to start you on antihypertensive medications. The decision whether or not to use medications is generally based on several factors, such as the level of your blood pressure, your age, and whether or not you have other risk factors.

The medications used in the treatment of hypertension are quite effective, and will reduce blood pressure level in most hypertensive patients. Because of their potency, however, these medications can cause bothersome side effects. Although they will lower blood pressure in most patients, they do not "cure" the disease. Due to the chronic nature of hypertension and its slow progression, treatment will almost certainly be lifelong.

Cutting Down on Salt

Salt is made up of sodium and chloride, two minerals that are essential in the maintenance of the body's fluid balance. The salt-fluid balance is controlled to a large degree by the kidneys. If an excessive amount of salt is taken, the kidneys may not be able to excrete the salt load, and as a result, the volume of fluid in the body gradually increases.

Salt, when consumed in excessive amounts, may cause an elevation of blood pressure in susceptible people. Studies have shown, for example, that adding salt to foods or eating foods high in salt are the factors that most likely contribute to the age-related tendency to develop hypertension. In patients with an already weakened heart, excessive salt intake may lead to accumulation of extra fluid in the body and symptoms of heart failure.

Most Americans consume more salt than their bodies need. After sugar, salt is our leading food additive. The average American consumes 10 to 15 grams of salt daily, the equivalent of 4 to 6 grams of sodium a day (one gram of salt contains 0.4 grams, or 400 milligrams, of sodium). The body's actual requirements are probably around 400 milligrams of sodium a day. To be on the safe side, the recommended daily allowance (RDA) for adults is 1,200 to 3,600 milligrams of sodium, or 3 to 8 grams of salt per day (one teaspoon is about 5 grams salt).

---

1 teaspoon salt = 5 grams salt = 2 grams sodium

*each gram contains 1,000 milligrams (mg)

When adding up the amount of salt you take, it is not enough to count only what is added to foods when cooking or at the table. Some sources of salt are obvious, such as salted crackers, nuts, pretzels, potato chips, pickles, herring, soy sauce, and sauerkraut. Other sources of salt, however, are less obvious or "hidden."

The major hidden source of salt comes from processed foods, which today account for over half of the food Americans eat. Salt and other sodium compounds are added to foods not only to make them taste better but also to improve color and texture and to preserve them. Among the processed foods containing a high level of sodium are: soups (especially canned soups), canned vegetables,

Shaking the Salt Habit

• Start by not adding salt at the table, and certainly never add salt before you have tasted the food.

• Gradually reduce the amount of salt you use in cooking and baking. As you get used to less and less salt, you will find you need to add only a fraction of the original amount.

• Clearly, the best way to avoid salt is to buy and cook as many fresh foods as possible. Fresh fruits, vegetables, meats, and unprocessed grains are generally low in sodium.

• Eat only limited amounts, or totally avoid, foods high in sodium such as: luncheon meats (salami, bologna), smoked meats (ham, bacon, sausage, corned beef), canned foods (soups, vegetables) that list high levels of salt on their labels, packaged bouillon, and certain condiments (catsup, chili sauce, mustard, and barbecue sauce).

• Experiment with seasonings, herbs, and spices, using them in place of salt. Examples: onions, garlic, pepper, dry mustard, lemon juice.

• How salty a food tastes is not necessarily a good indicator of how much sodium it contains. If you are on a sodium-restricted diet, check the label on all processed foods for sodium content. If you are dependent on processed foods, look for those labeled "low sodium" or "low salt."

• Watch out for commercially prepared condiments, sauces, and seasonings. Many are high in sodium, like onion salt, garlic salt, seasoned salt, meat tenderizer, bouillon, soy sauce, steak sauce, barbecue sauce, catsup, mustard, worcestershire sauce, salad dressings, pickles, chili sauce, and relish.

• Examples of sodium-containing ingredients and their uses in foods: baking powder and baking soda (leavening agents),

Continued

monosodium glutamate (flavor enhancer), sodium benzoate (preservative), and sodium nitrite (curing agent in meat).

• If you are on sodium restricted diet, check with your doctor before taking antacids, cough preparations, and laxatives. Many of these items contain a significant amount of sodium.

cheese, luncheon meats, cereals, baked goods, bread, pancakes, and pudding. These products are heavily laced with salt as well as other sources of sodium.

By simply avoiding foods that are high in sodium, and by not using the salt shaker at the table, most people can reduce their overall salt intake and thus lower their risk of high blood pressure. Additional sodium restriction is generally recommended in patients with high blood pressure and for those with heart failure.

Reading the Label

Placing sodium content on the nutrition label is now optional, unless the product claims to be low or reduced in sodium, or to have less salt or no salt added. However, many manufacturers are providing this information as a service to consumers.

Sodium on nutrition labels is given in milligrams (mg) per serving. This includes sodium naturally present in the ingredients as well as sodium added during processing. Salt is the major, but not the only, source of sodium in food products. Any ingredient that has sodium, salt, or soda as part of its name (such as monosodium glutamate, seasoned salt, and baking soda) contains sodium.

Many manufacturers are introducing foods with reduced sodium. Examples of types of foods that are now available in low-sodium form or with reduced or no added salt include: canned vegetables, vegetable juices, and sauces; canned soups; dried soup mixes, bouillon; condiments; snack foods (chips, nuts, pretzels); ready-to-eat cereals; bread, bakery products; butter, margarine; cheeses; tuna; processed meats. Look for reduced-sodium versions of these products when you shop.

What about Salt Substitutes?

Salt substitutes are not for everyone, but they may be helpful for some people trying to reduce their sodium intake. Many salt substitutes contain potassium in place of all or part of the sodium. People under medical supervision, particularly for kidney problems, should check with their physician before using these salt substitutes.

Some salt substitutes contain neither sodium nor potassium, but instead are mixtures of spices and herbs. These, as well as homemade seasoning blends, can be used to flavor foods without added sodium.

16 Making It Work— It's Up to You

By completing this book, you've already taken an important step toward a healthier lifestyle. But just reading a book isn't enough—you've got to get out there and do it! The following ten steps will help you put the knowledge you have gained into practice and will guide you toward achieving your goal of lower cholesterol and a healthier heart.

1) Know Your Numbers

Have your cholesterol checked. The easiest way is to do it as part of your routine physical. Another way is to have it checked at a screening site in your community. Ask for the actual number and not just if it's "normal." And remember: if your cholesterol is too high, you have a greater risk of developing heart disease.

Another important number you should know is your daily fat allowance—the amount of fat you are allowed to consume each day. It takes only a few minutes to determine. It is based on your weight, your activity level, and your gender. (See Chapter 7). By knowing your fat limit, you'll have a better understanding of what to eat and what to avoid each day.

2) Learn to Make the Right Choices

When you go grocery shopping, start thinking about how to make sensible selections within the five basic food groups (bread and cereals; fruits and vegetables; milk and dairy products; meat, poultry, and fish; fats and oils). In each category, choose those foods that are lower in fat, especially saturated fats, lower in cholesterol, and lower in added sugar and salt. Emphasize foods rich in complex carbohydrates and fiber. In the kitchen, choose cooking methods that use little or no fat, such as steaming, baking, or broiling.

You can enjoy dining out and still stay within your fat and cholesterol "budget." The secret is, once again, in selecting the right foods and the right food preparations. For your entree, your best choices are chicken and seafood. Lean red meats, when properly trimmed and prepared, are also acceptable. Choose food preparations described in terms suggestive of low-fat preparation (such as broiled, roasted, or poached). Side dishes of vegetables and starches (potatoes, pasta, rice) are good complements to your meal, but choose those cooked with little or no fat, rather than fried or covered with sauce or cream.

3) Be an Informed Consumer

Learn to read the label! Reading food labels and understanding the information on them will assist you in making wiser food choices. And don't forget to practice what you've learned. When you go grocery shopping, spend some extra time and practice reading labels. Remember that some of the bold claims you read on the labels—although not untruthful—can be misleading. As a consumer, you should learn to interpret those claims. Food tables, which list the fat and cholesterol content of various foods, can also be very useful. No one is expected to memorize the breakdown of each and every food, but you'll soon start picking up on trends.

4) Use Moderation and Common Sense

Unless you have a specific health problem that requires you to avoid certain foods, there is no reason why you have to totally give up foods you especially enjoy. There is nothing wrong with ice cream (or a salami sandwich) once or twice a week. It's often a question of tradeoffs—if you eat a high-fat food for one meal, choose those low in fat for the rest of your meals that day.

Remember that having too much of a good thing is not necessarily good for you. Don't start eating large amounts of oat bran while neglecting other healthy sources of dietary fiber such as dried beans, fruits, and vegetables. Also, control the size of your portions. If you eat a half-pound steak at a sitting, you'll be taking in too much fat and cholesterol and you'll exceed your fat and cholesterol budget for the day.

5) *Change Your Habits Gradually*

Changes in your eating habits should be gradual. Gradual changes are easier to adapt to and more likely to last. If you've been drinking whole milk all your life, try switching to low-fat 2% milk for a few weeks, then to low-fat 1% milk, and finally to skim milk. This way, you'll have a chance to get accustomed to the taste.

If you are overweight and need to reduce, don't try to shed those extra pounds too rapidly. Although you may tolerate a severe restriction in your diet for a while, eventually you'll likely give in to hunger and the limits on your lifestyle, and regain whatever weight you may have lost.

6) *Get More Exercise*

Choose an aerobic activity performed at a level appropriate for you, for a period of 20 to 30 minutes, 3 to 4 times a week. Good aerobic activities include brisk walking, jogging, running, swimming, and bicycling. The type of exercise(s) you choose should provide you with some enjoyment, so you can continue with it for years to come.

Start slowly and increase speed, distance, and duration in a gradual manner. Warm up thoroughly prior to the workout and cool down following it. And remember to consult your doctor prior to starting an exercise program, especially if you are over 40, not accustomed to vigorous exercise, or have any health problems that may increase your risk.

7) *Don't Forget the Other Factors*

Other factors, such as smoking and high blood pressure, also increase your risk of heart disease. It doesn't make any sense to try so hard to lower your cholesterol if, at the same time, you continue smoking or ignore your high blood pressure. If you smoke, now is the time to kick the habit. Remember also that high blood pressure doesn't cause any symptoms during its early stages (it is "silent"). So, have your blood pressure checked periodically, and if it's elevated, take the proper measures to lower it, such as cutting down on salt, losing weight, and exercising regularly.

8) Don't Hesitate to Get Some Help

If you have not achieved your cholesterol goal after a few months on a sensible diet, it's probably time to get some help. Discuss the matter with your doctor. He or she will give you some additional instructions and will provide you with the support and encouragement you need. Your doctor may refer you to a registered dietitian. With the help of the dietitian, you will resume your diet under supervision, or you may be put on a stricter diet program. If you have been referred to a dietitian, it's important that you continue with regular follow-ups, at least until you have acquired new eating habits and feel you are in control of things.

9) Keep at It for a Lifetime

If you follow the program prescribed in this book, you'll most likely lower your blood cholesterol and reach your cholesterol goal. You must realize, however, that this plan is not a "cure" for your cholesterol problem. Rather, it is a new way of living. If you want to be successful in controlling your cholesterol you must keep at it, not just for eight weeks, not just for a year, but for the rest of your life. The reward is worth it. Soon, you'll be shopping for healthier foods, losing weight without feeling deprived, getting more exercise, and having more fun.

10) Take Action—Today!

If you have a cholesterol problem, now is the time to take action to lower it. Change your eating habits! Keep those extra pounds off! Get more exercise into your life!

And whatever action you take, remember that *you* are in charge. Your doctor and dietitian are there to guide you and monitor your progress, but it's up to you to make it work. Remember also that when you take action to lower your cholesterol you will reduce your risk of heart disease and, most importantly, you will increase your chances of living a long, active, and healthy life.

Appendix

Food Tables

Fat and Cholesterol Content of Common Foods

The following table was compiled from a number of sources including publications from the U.S. Department of Agriculture (such as the *USDA Home and Garden Bulletin Number 72, Nutritive value of Foods*), the National Institute of Health, and the American Heart Association.

Values for fat have been rounded off to the nearest gram. An asterisk appears when the value reported is less than one gram. Values for calories, cholesterol, and sodium have been rounded off to the nearest ten.

The table is arranged by food category, and foods are listed alphabetically within each category. The following list should help you locate a specific category more easily.

	Calories Cals.	**Total fat** Grams	**Saturated fat** Grams	**Cholesterol** Milligrams	**Sodium** Milligrams

DAIRY PRODUCTS and EGGS

Cheese

	Calories Cals.	**Total fat** Grams	**Saturated fat** Grams	**Cholesterol** Milligrams	**Sodium** Milligrams
American, processed (1 oz)	110	9	6	30	410
Blue (1 oz)	100	8	5	20	400
Brick (1 oz)	110	8	5	30	160
Brie (1 oz)	100	8	5	30	180
Camembert (1 oz)	90	7	4	20	240
Cheddar (1 oz)	110	9	6	30	180
Colby (1 oz)	110	9	6	30	170
Cottage cheese (1/2 cup):					
Creamed	120	5	3	20	460
Low fat 2%	100	2	1	10	460
Low fat 1%	80	1	1	5	460
Dry curd	60	*	*	5	10
Cream cheese (1 oz)	100	10	6	30	80
Cream cheese, "light" (1 oz)	60	5	3	20	160
Edam (1 oz)	100	8	5	30	270
Feta (1 oz)	80	6	4	30	320
Gouda (1 oz)	100	8	5	30	230
Gruyère (1 oz)	120	9	5	30	100
Monterey Jack (1 oz)	110	9	5	30	150

* Less than 1

	Calories Cals.	Total fat Grams	Saturated fat Grams	Cholesterol Milligrams	Sodium Milligrams
Mozzarella, part-skim milk (1 oz)	70	5	3	20	150
Mozzarella, whole milk (1 oz)	80	6	4	20	110
Muenster (1 oz)	100	8	5	30	180
Neufchatel (1 oz)	70	7	4	20	110
Parmesan, grated (1 oz)	130	9	5	20	530
Provolone (1 oz)	100	8	5	20	250
Ricotta, part-skim milk (1/2 cup)	170	10	6	40	150
Ricotta, whole milk (1/2 cup)	210	16	10	60	100
Romano (1 oz)	110	8	5	30	340
Roquefort (1 oz)	110	9	6	30	510
Swiss (1 oz)	110	8	5	30	70
Swiss, processed (1 oz)	100	7	5	20	390

Cheese Products

	Calories Cals.	Total fat Grams	Saturated fat Grams	Cholesterol Milligrams	Sodium Milligrams
American cheese food (1 oz)	90	7	4	20	340
American cheese spread (1 oz)	80	6	4	20	380

Cream

	Calories Cals.	Total fat Grams	Saturated fat Grams	Cholesterol Milligrams	Sodium Milligrams
Half and half cream (1 tbsp)	20	2	1	10	10
Light cream, coffee or table (1 tbsp)	30	3	2	10	10
Whipped cream, pressurized (1 tbsp)	10	1	*	5	10
Sour cream, real (1 tbsp)	30	3	2	10	10

* Less than 1

	Calories Cals.	Total fat Grams	Saturated fat Grams	Cholesterol Milligrams	Sodium Milligrams
Cream Substitutes					
Nondairy creamer, liquid (1 tbsp)	20	2	1	0	10
Nondairy creamer, powder (1 teaspoon)	10	1	1	0	0
Dessert topping, frozen (1 tbsp)	20	1	1	0	0
Sour cream, imitation (1 tbsp)	30	3	2	0	10
Milk					
Milk (1 cup):					
Whole milk	150	8	5	30	120
Low fat 2%	120	5	3	20	120
Low fat 1%	100	3	2	10	120
Skim (nonfat)	90	*	*	5	130
Condensed, sweetened, canned (1 fl oz)	120	3	2	10	50
Evaporated, whole, canned (1 fl oz)	40	2	2	10	30
Evaporated, skim, canned (1 fl oz)	30	0	0	0	40
Buttermilk (1 cup)	100	2	1	10	260
Milk Beverages					
Chocolate milk, whole milk (1 cup)	210	8	5	30	150
Chocolate milk, low fat 2% (1 cup)	180	5	3	20	150
Hot chocolate, whole milk (1 cup)	220	9	6	30	120
Milk shake, chocolate (1 cup)	290	9	5	30	220

* Less than 1

	Calories Cals.	Total fat Grams	Saturated fat Grams	Cholesterol Milligrams	Sodium Milligrams
Yogurt					
Regular, plain (1 cup)	140	7	5	30	110
Low fat, plain (1 cup)	140	4	2	10	160
Low fat, fruit flavor (1 cup)	230	3	2	10	120
Nonfat, plain (1 cup)	130	*	*	5	170
Milk Desserts					
Custard, baked (1/2 cup)	150	7	3	140	100
Pudding (1/2 cup)	170	4	2	20	440
Frozen Desserts					
(see page 183)					
Eggs					
Whole egg (1 large)	80	6	2	250	70
Egg white	20	0	0	0	50
Egg yolk	60	6	2	250	10
Egg substitute (1/4 cup):					
Liquid (check label—several are fat free)	50	2	0	0	40
Frozen	100	7	1	0	120

* Less than 1

MEAT, POULTRY, and FISH

Beef

	Calories Cals.	Total fat Grams	Saturated fat Grams	Cholesterol Milligrams	Sodium Milligrams
Brisket, braised (3 oz):					
Lean and fat	340	28	11	80	50
Lean only	210	11	4	80	60
Chuck blade roast, braised (3 oz):					
Lean and fat	330	26	11	90	50
Lean only	230	13	5	90	60
Flank steak, braised (3 oz):					
Lean and fat	220	13	6	60	60
Lean only	210	12	5	60	60
Rib, roasted (3 oz):					
Lean and fat	330	27	11	70	50
Lean only	210	12	5	70	60
Shortribs, braised (3 oz):					
Lean and fat	400	36	15	80	40
Lean only	250	16	7	80	50
Bottom round, braised (3 oz):					
Lean and fat	220	13	5	80	40
Lean only	190	8	3	80	40

	Calories Cals.	Total fat Grams	Saturated fat Grams	Cholesterol Milligrams	Sodium Milligrams
Eye of round, roasted (3 oz):					
Lean and fat	210	12	5	60	50
Lean only	160	6	2	60	50
Porterhouse steak, broiled (3 oz):					
Lean and fat	260	18	8	70	50
Lean only	190	9	4	70	60
T-bone steak, broiled (3 oz):					
Lean and fat	280	21	9	70	50
Lean only	180	9	4	70	60
Sirloin, broiled (3 oz):					
Lean and fat	240	15	6	80	50
Lean only	180	7	3	80	60
Ground beef, broiled (3 oz):					
Regular	250	18	7	80	70
Lean	230	16	6	70	70
Extra lean	220	14	5	70	60
Variety meats (3 oz):					
Brain, simmered	140	11	2	1,760	100
Heart, simmered	150	5	1	170	50
Liver, braised	140	4	2	330	60
Tongue, simmered	240	18	8	90	50

	Calories Cals.	Total fat Grams	Saturated fat Grams	Cholesterol Milligrams	Sodium Milligrams
Lamb					
Loin chop, broiled (3 oz):					
Lean and fat	310	25	14	70	50
Lean only	160	6	4	70	60
Leg, roasted (3 oz):					
Lean and fat	240	16	9	80	50
Lean only	160	6	3	80	60
Rib, roasted (3 oz):					
Lean and fat	350	30	17	100	40
Lean only	180	9	5	150	60
Shoulder, roasted (3 oz):					
Lean and fat	290	23	13	100	50
Lean only	170	9	5	100	60
Cutlet, grilled (3 oz)	190	9	5	90	60
Pork					
Loin chop, broiled (3 oz):					
Lean and fat	300	23	8	80	60
Lean only	220	13	5	80	60
Leg, roasted (3 oz):					
Lean and fat	250	18	6	80	50
Lean only	190	9	3	80	50

	Calories Cals.	Total fat Grams	Saturated fat Grams	Cholesterol Milligrams	Sodium Milligrams
Rib, roasted (3 oz):					
Lean and fat	270	20	7	70	40
Lean only	210	12	4	70	40
Shoulder, roasted (3 oz):					
Lean and fat	280	22	8	80	60
Lean only	210	13	4	80	70
Ham, lean, roasted (3 oz)	120	5	2	50	1,030
Spareribs, braised (3 oz)	340	26	10	100	80
Bacon, pan fried (1 oz)	160	14	5	20	450
Breakfast strips, cooked (1 oz)	130	10	4	30	590
Canadian-style bacon, grilled (2 oz)	100	5	2	30	860
Veal					
Cutlet, broiled (3 oz)	190	9	4	110	60
Loin, broiled (3 oz)	200	11	6	80	60
Rib, roasted (3 oz)	230	14	7	110	60

Luncheon Meats and Sausages

	Calories Cals.	Total fat Grams	Saturated fat Grams	Cholesterol Milligrams	Sodium Milligrams
Bologna, beef (2 oz)	180	16	7	30	550
Bologna, turkey (2 oz)	120	9	3	40	440
Chicken roll (2 oz)	90	4	1	30	330
Corned beef loaf (2 oz)	90	3	1	30	540
Frankfurter, beef (2 oz)	180	16	7	40	590
Frankfurter, turkey (2 oz)	120	10	3	50	590
Ham, cured (2 oz)	100	6	2	30	750
Italian sausage, pork (2 oz)	180	14	5	40	520
Kielbasa (2 oz)	170	15	6	40	600
Knockwurst sausage (2 oz)	170	16	6	30	570
Pastrami, beef (2 oz)	200	17	6	50	700
Pastrami, turkey (2 oz)	80	4	1	30	590
Pepperoni (1 oz)	130	11	4	20	520
Polish sausage, pork (2 oz)	180	16	6	40	500
Pork liver sausage (2 oz)	200	18	6	90	640
Salami, dry, beef and pork (2 oz)	240	19	7	40	1,040
Salami, turkey (2 oz)	110	8	2	50	570
Sandwich spread (beef, pork) (2 oz)	130	10	3	20	570
Sandwich spread (chicken, turkey) (2 oz)	110	6	1	20	210
Smoked link sausage (2 oz)	190	17	8	40	530
Turkey roll (2 oz)	80	4	1	30	330

	Calories Cals.	Total fat Grams	Saturated fat Grams	Cholesterol Milligrams	Sodium Milligrams
Chicken					
Dark meat, roasted (3 oz):					
With skin	220	14	4	80	70
Without skin	180	8	2	80	80
Dark meat, fried (3 oz):					
With skin	240	14	4	80	80
Without skin	200	10	3	80	80
Light meat, roasted (3 oz):					
With skin	190	9	3	70	60
Without skin	150	4	1	70	70
Light meat, fried (3 oz):					
With skin	210	10	3	70	70
Without skin	160	5	1	80	70
Breast, fried (1/2 breast):					
With skin	220	9	2	90	80
Without skin	160	4	1	80	70
Leg, fried (1 leg):					
With skin	290	16	4	110	100
Without skin	190	8	2	90	80
Giblets (gizzard, heart, liver) (3 oz)	130	4	1	340	50

	Calories Cals.	Total fat Grams	Saturated fat Grams	Cholesterol Milligrams	Sodium Milligrams
Turkey					
Dark meat, roasted (3 oz):					
With skin	190	10	3	80	70
Without skin	160	6	2	70	70
Light meat, roasted (3 oz):					
With skin	170	7	2	70	50
Without skin	130	3	1	60	50
Ground turkey (3 oz)	180	11	4	70	90
Fish					
Bass (3 oz)	80	2	*	70	60
Bluefish (3 oz)	110	4	1	50	50
Cod (3 oz)	90	1	0	50	70
Fish fillet (3 oz)	180	10	3	80	230
Fish sticks (3 oz)	230	10	3	90	490
Flounder/sole (3 oz)	60	*	0	50	50
Haddock (3 oz)	100	1	0	60	70
Halibut (3 oz)	120	3	*	40	60
Herring (3 oz)	170	10	2	70	100
Herring, pickled (1 oz)	70	5	1	5	240
Ocean perch (3 oz)	100	2	*	50	80
Orange roughy (3 oz)	110	6	*	20	50

* Less than 1

	Calories Cals.	Total fat Grams	Saturated fat Grams	Cholesterol Milligrams	Sodium Milligrams
Pollock (3 oz)	80	1	0	60	70
Salmon, Atlantic (3 oz)	120	5	1	50	40
Salmon, pink, canned (3 oz)	120	5	1	40	470
Sardines, canned in oil (2 oz)	120	7	1	80	280
Snapper (3 oz)	110	2	*	40	50
Sole (see flounder)					
Swordfish (3 oz)	130	4	1	40	100
Trout (3 oz)	130	4	1	60	30
Tuna, packed in oil (3 oz)	170	7	1	20	300
Tuna, packed in water (3 oz)	110	*	0	20	300
Shellfish					
Clam (3 oz)	130	2	*	60	100
Crab, Alaska king (3 oz)	80	1	0	50	910
Lobster (3 oz)	80	1	0	60	320
Oysters, raw (3 oz)	70	2	*	50	90
Scallops (3 oz)	80	1	0	30	140
Shrimp, cooked (3 oz)	80	1	0	170	190
Shrimp, fried (3 oz)	190	9	2	100	160

* Less than 1

GRAIN PRODUCTS

	Calories Cals.	Total fat Grams	Saturated fat Grams	Cholesterol Milligrams	Sodium Milligrams
Breads					
Cracked wheat bread (1 slice)	70	1	*	0	110
French bread (1 slice)	80	1	*	0	190
Italian bread (1 slice)	80	1	*	0	150
Mixed grain bread (1 slice)	60	1	*	0	100
Oatmeal bread (1 slice)	70	1	*	0	140
Pita bread (1 pocket)	110	1	*	0	220
Pumpernickel (1 slice)	80	1	*	0	173
Raisin bread (1 slice)	70	1	*	0	100
Rye bread (1 slice)	70	1	*	0	170
Sourdough (1 slice)	70	1	*	0	140
Wheat bread (1 slice)	60	1	*	0	130
White bread (1 slice)	60	1	*	0	120
Whole-wheat bread (1 slice)	60	1	*	0	160
Baked Goods					
Bagel (1)	160	1	0	0	200
Biscuit, from mix (1)	90	3	1	0	260
Bread crumbs (1 cup)	390	5	1	5	740
Bread stuffing, from mix (1/2 cup)	210	13	7	0	500

* Less than 1

	Calories Cals.	Total fat Grams	Saturated fat Grams	Cholesterol Milligrams	Sodium Milligrams
Corn bread, from mix (1 piece)	180	6	2	0	260
Croissant (1)	240	12	4	10	450
Danish pastry (1)	160	9	3	40	160
Doughnut (1)	210	12	3	20	190
English muffin (1)	140	1	0	0	360
French toast, homemade (1 slice)	150	7	2	110	260
Muffin, blueberry or bran (1)	130	4	1	50	200
Pancake, homemade, 4" diam. (1)	60	2	*	20	120
Roll or bun (1)	90	2	*	0	160
Taco shell (1)	60	2	*	0	60
Toaster pastry (1)	210	6	2	0	250
Tortilla, corn (1)	70	1	0	0	50
Tortilla, flour (1)	90	2	*	0	160
Waffle, from mix, 7" diam. (1)	210	8	3	60	520

Breakfast Cereals

Cereals, cooked (1 cup):					
Corn grits	150	1	0	0	0
Cream of rice	130	*	0	0	10
Cream of wheat	140	1	0	0	10
Oatmeal (rolled oats)	150	2	*	0	0
Whole wheat	150	1	0	0	0

* Less than 1

Cereals, ready-to-eat (1 oz):	Calories Cals.	Total fat Grams	Saturated fat Grams	Cholesterol Milligrams	Sodium Milligrams
All Bran	70	1	0	0	320
Bran flakes	90	1	0	0	260
Cheerios	110	2	*	0	290
Corn flakes	110	*	0	0	350
Crackling Oat Bran	110	4	1	0	230
Fiber One	60	1	0	0	230
Fruit and Fiber	90	1	0	0	190
Granola, Nature Valley	130	5	3	0	60
Grapenuts	100	*	0	0	190
Nutri-Grain	100	*	0	0	190
Product 19	110	*	0	0	330
Puffed cereal, rice or wheat	110	*	0	0	20
Quaker 100% natural	140	6	4	0	10
Raisin bran	90	1	0	0	210
Rice Chex	110	*	0	0	250
Rice Krispies	110	*	0	0	340
Shredded Wheat	100	1	0	0	0
Special K	110	*	0	0	270
Total	100	1	0	0	280
Wheat Chex	100	1	0	0	200
Wheaties	100	1	0	0	270

* Less than 1

	Calories Cals.	Total fat Grams	Saturated fat Grams	Cholesterol Milligrams	Sodium Milligrams
Pasta and Rice					
Egg noodles (1 cup, cooked)	200	2	*	50	0
Macaroni (1 cup, cooked)	160	1	0	0	0
Spaghetti (1 cup, cooked)	160	1	0	0	0
Rice, white or brown (1 cup, cooked)	220	*	0	0	0
Grains					
Barley (1 cup, cooked)	200	1	0	0	0
Corn meal (1 cup, cooked)	120	1	0	0	0
Oat bran (1/3 cup)	60	1	0	0	10
Rolled wheat (1 cup, cooked)	140	1	0	0	0
Wheat bran (1/2 cup)	40	1	0	0	0
Wheat flour (1 cup)	420	1	0	0	0
Wheat germ, toasted (1 cup)	430	12	2	0	0
Whole-grain wheat (1/3 cup, cooked)	30	1	0	0	0

* Less than 1

	Calories Cals.	Total fat Grams	Saturated fat Grams	Cholesterol Milligrams	Sodium Milligrams
STARCHY VEGETABLES and NUTS					
Starchy Vegetables					
Beans, canned (1 cup)	210	1	0	0	890
Corn, canned (1 cup)	170	1	0	0	570
Garbanzo beans, cooked (1 cup)	270	4	*	0	10
Lentils, cooked (1 cup)	230	1	0	0	0
Peas, cooked (1 cup)	180	1	0	0	10
Potatoes:					
Baked (1 potato)	210	*	0	0	20
French fries (3 oz)	270	14	4	0	180
Mashed, with milk and butter (1 cup)	240	12	7	5	700
Soybeans, cooked from dry (1 cup)	300	15	2	0	0
Soybean products (1/2 cup):					
Miso	280	8	1	0	5,030
Tofu	90	6	1	0	10
Sweet potato, cooked (1)	120	1	0	0	10
Nuts and Seeds * *					
Almonds (1 oz)	170	15	1	0	0
Brazilnuts (1 oz)	190	19	5	0	0
Cashews (1 oz)	160	13	3	0	0

* Less than 1   * * Unsalted

	Calories Cals.	Total fat Grams	Saturated fat Grams	Cholesterol Milligrams	Sodium Milligrams
European chestnuts (1 cup)	350	3	*	0	0
Filberts (hazelnuts) (1 oz)	180	18	1	0	0
Macadamia nuts (1 oz)	200	22	3	0	0
Peanuts (1 oz)	160	14	2	0	10
Pecans (1 oz)	190	19	2	0	0
Pine nuts (1 oz)	160	17	3	0	20
Pistachio nuts, shelled (1 oz)	160	14	2	0	0
Pumpkin seeds (1 oz)	150	13	3	0	10
Sesame seeds (1 oz)	220	21	3	0	20
Sunflower seed kernels (1/4 cup)	210	18	2	0	0
Walnuts, black (1 oz)	170	16	1	0	0
Walnuts, English (1 oz)	180	18	2	0	0

* Less than 1

SOUPS, SAUCES, and GRAVIES

	Calories Cals.	Total fat Grams	Saturated fat Grams	Cholesterol Milligrams	Sodium Milligrams
Soups — Canned, Condensed					
Prepared with equal volume of whole milk (1 cup):					
Clam chowder, New England	160	7	3	20	990
Cream of celery	170	10	4	30	1,010
Cream of chicken	190	12	5	30	1,050
Cream of mushroom	210	14	5	20	1,080
Cream of potato	150	6	4	20	1,060
Oyster stew	130	8	5	30	1,040
Tomato	160	6	3	20	930
Prepared with equal volume of water (1 cup):					
Bean with bacon	170	6	2	5	950
Beef noodle	80	3	1	10	950
Chicken noodle (or rice)	80	2	*	10	900
Chili beef soup	170	7	3	10	1,040
Clam chowder, Manhattan	80	2	*	5	1,810
Cream of chicken	120	7	2	10	990
Cream of mushroom	130	9	2	0	1,030
Minestrone	80	3	1	0	910
Onion soup	60	2	*	0	1,050
Split pea with ham	190	4	2	10	1,010

* Less than 1

	Calories Cals.	Total fat Grams	Saturated fat Grams	Cholesterol Milligrams	Sodium Milligrams
Tomato rice	90	2	*	0	870
Vegetable beef	80	2	1	10	960
Vegetarian vegetable	70	2	*	0	820

Soups — Dehydrated, prepared with water (1 cup)

Beef broth	20	1	0	0	1,360
Chicken broth	20	1	0	0	1,480
Chicken noodle	50	1	0	5	1,280
Cream of chicken	110	5	3	5	1,180
Onion	30	1	0	0	850
Split pea	130	2	*	5	1,220
Tomato vegetable	50	1	0	0	1,140

Sauces

From dry mixes, prepared with milk (1/4 cup):

Bernaise	180	17	10	50	320
Cheese sauce	80	4	2	10	390
Hollandaise	60	5	3	10	390
Mushroom	60	3	1	10	380
Stroganoff	70	3	2	10	460
White sauce	60	3	2	10	200

* Less than 1

	Calories Cals.	Total fat Grams	Saturated fat Grams	Cholesterol Milligrams	Sodium Milligrams
Ready to serve (1 tbsp):					
Barbecue sauce	10	*	0	0	130
Soy sauce	10	0	0	0	1,030
Teriyaki sauce	20	*	0	0	690
Spaghetti sauce, canned (1/2 cup)	110	3	0	0	500
Gravies					
Canned (1/4 cup):					
Au jus	10	0	0	0	150
Beef	30	1	*	5	30
Chicken	50	3	1	5	340
Mushroom	30	2	*	0	340
Turkey	30	1	*	5	340
From dry mix, prepared with water (1/4 cup):					
Au jus	10	0	0	0	150
Brown	20	0	0	0	30
Chicken	20	1	0	5	280
Mushroom	20	0	0	0	350
Onion	20	0	0	0	260
Turkey	20	1	0	5	380

* Less than 1

	Calories Cals.	Total fat Grams	Saturated fat Grams	Cholesterol Milligrams	Sodium Milligrams
DESSERTS and SNACKS					
Frozen Desserts					
Frozen yogurt, low fat (1/2 cup)	120	2	2	10	60
Frozen yogurt, nonfat (1/2 cup)	130	*	0	10	60
Ice cream, rich (1/2 cup)	270	17	11	60	60
Ice cream, regular (1/2 cup)	270	14	9	60	120
Ice milk (1/2 cup)	90	3	2	10	50
Sherbet (1/2 cup)	140	2	1	10	40
Sorbet (1/2 cup)	110	0	0	0	10
Popsicle (1 bar)	70	0	0	0	10
Cakes					
Angel food cake (1 piece, 2 oz)	130	1	0	0	280
Boston cream pie (1 piece, 3 oz)	180	6	2	10	160
Cheesecake (1 piece, 3 oz)	260	17	9	160	190
Coffee cake (1 piece, 3 oz)	270	8	2	60	370
Cupcake (1 piece, 2 oz)	190	7	2	5	280
Devil's food (1 piece, 2 oz)	190	6	3	30	150
Fruitcake (1 piece, 2 oz)	210	9	2	30	90
Gingerbread (1 piece, 2 oz)	150	4	1	0	170
Pound cake (1 piece, 2 oz)	220	9	2	60	180

* Less than 1

	Calories Cals.	Total fat Grams	Saturated fat Grams	Cholesterol Milligrams	Sodium Milligrams
White cake (1 piece, 3 oz)	310	11	3	5	210
Yellow cake (1 piece, 3 oz)	300	14	7	50	240
Cake frosting, chocolate (1/4 cup)	260	10	5	5	40
Cake frosting, white (1/4 cup)	300	5	3	5	40
Pies					
Apple (1 piece, 4 oz)	290	13	3	0	340
Banana cream (1 piece, 4 oz)	180	7	3	10	240
Blueberry (1 piece, 4 oz)	270	12	3	0	300
Cherry (1 piece, 4 oz)	290	13	3	0	340
Chocolate cream (1 piece, 4 oz)	200	8	3	10	270
Custard (1 piece, 4 oz)	220	10	1	110	250
Lemon meringue (1 piece, 4 oz)	280	11	3	110	320
Peach (1 piece, 4 oz)	290	12	3	0	300
Pecan (1 piece, 4 oz)	470	19	3	110	250
Pumpkin (1 piece, 4 oz)	270	12	4	80	250
Pie crust, baked (1 oz)	140	9	2	0	170
Cookies					
Animal crackers (2 oz)	240	5	1	30	170
Brownies, with nuts (2 oz)	270	18	4	40	140
Butter cookies (2 oz)	260	10	3	30	230

	Calories Cals.	Total fat Grams	Saturated fat Grams	Cholesterol Milligrams	Sodium Milligrams
Chocolate chip (2 oz)	260	12	4	40	220
Fig bars (2 oz)	210	4	1	60	180
Gingersnaps (2 oz)	240	5	1	60	320
Macaroons (2 oz)	270	13	6	10	20
Oatmeal raisin (2 oz)	250	9	2	5	90
Peanut butter cookies (2 oz)	280	14	4	20	190
Sandwich-type cookies (2 oz)	280	13	3	20	270
Shortbread cookies (2 oz)	280	13	3	60	30
Sugar cookies (2 oz)	250	9	2	50	180
Vanilla wafers (2 oz)	260	9	3	40	140
Crackers					
Armenian cracker bread (1 oz)	120	2	*	0	100
Bread sticks (1 oz)	110	1	0	0	200
Cheese crackers (1 oz)	140	8	3	20	310
Graham crackers (1 oz)	120	2	*	0	170
Matzo (1 oz)	120	*	0	0	10
Melba toast (1 oz)	110	3	1	0	250
Oyster crackers (1 oz)	120	4	1	0	290
Rye wafers (1 oz)	110	2	1	0	230
Saltine crackers (1 oz)	120	2	1	10	390
Snack-type crackers (1 oz)	140	9	2	0	280

* Less than 1

	Calories Cals.	Total fat Grams	Saturated fat Grams	Cholesterol Milligrams	Sodium Milligrams
Wheat crackers, thin (1 oz)	120	4	2	0	240
Whole-wheat wafers (1 oz)	120	7	2	0	210
Zwieback (1 oz)	120	2	1	0	70
Chips and Other Snacks					
Cheese balls (1 oz)	160	11	3	0	280
Corn chips (1 oz)	150	9	2	0	220
Potato chips (1 oz)	150	10	3	0	130
Pretzels (1 oz)	110	1	0	0	450
Tortilla chips (1 oz)	150	8	2	0	160
Popcorn (2 cups):					
Air popped	50	*	0	0	0
Butter & salt added	80	4	2	0	350
Microwave, frozen	130	8	3	0	180
Sweets					
Candy corn (1 oz)	100	1	0	0	60
Caramel candy (1 oz)	120	3	2	0	60
Chocolate, plain (1 oz)	150	9	5	10	20
Chocolate, with almonds (1 oz)	150	10	4	10	20
Chocolate candies, plain (1 oz)	140	6	3	0	20
Chocolate candies, with peanuts (1 oz)	140	7	3	0	20

* Less than 1

	Calories Cals.	Total fat Grams	Saturated fat Grams	Cholesterol Milligrams	Sodium Milligrams
Chocolate fudge (1 oz)	120	3	2	0	50
Gelatine dessert (1/2 cup)	70	0	0	0	60
Gumdrops (1 oz)	100	*	0	0	10
Hard candy (1 oz)	110	0	0	0	10
Jelly beans (1 oz)	100	0	0	0	10
Marshmallows (1 oz)	90	0	0	0	30
Honey (1 tbsp)	70	0	0	0	0
Jam, jelly (1 tbsp)	50	0	0	0	0
Pancake syrup, maple (1/4 cup)	240	0	0	0	40
Sugar (1 tbsp)	50	0	0	0	0

* Less than 1

FATS and OILS

	Calories Cals.	Total fat Grams	Saturated fat Grams	Cholesterol Milligrams	Sodium Milligrams
Animal Fats (1 tbsp)					
Butter	100	12	7	30	120
Beef fat/tallow	120	13	6	10	0
Chicken fat	120	13	4	10	0
Lard (pork fat)	120	13	5	10	0
Vegetable Fats					
Vegetable shortening (1 tbsp)	110	12	3	0	0
Margarine (1 tbsp):					
Stick	100	11	3	0	130
Tub	100	11	2	0	150
Imitation (diet)	50	6	1	0	140
Vegetable oils (1 tbsp):					
Canola	120	14	1	0	0
Coconut	120	14	12	0	0
Corn	120	14	2	0	0
Cottonseed	120	14	4	0	0
Olive	120	14	2	0	0
Palm	120	14	7	0	0
Peanut	120	14	2	0	0

	Calories Cals.	Total fat Grams	Saturated fat Grams	Cholesterol Milligrams	Sodium Milligrams
Safflower	120	14	1	0	0
Soybean	120	14	2	0	0
Sunflower	120	14	1	0	0

Salad Dressings

Salad dressing, regular (1 tbsp)

	Calories	Total fat	Saturated fat	Cholesterol	Sodium
Blue cheese	80	8	1	0	160
French	70	6	1	0	210
Italian	70	7	1	0	120
Mayonnaise type	60	5	*	5	110
Thousand Island	60	6	1	0	110
Vinegar and oil	70	8	1	0	0

Salad dressing, low cal. (1 tbsp):

French	20	1	0	0	130
Italian	20	2	*	0	120
Thousand Island	20	2	*	0	150

Mayonnaise (1 tbsp):

Regular	100	11	2	10	80
"Light"	50	5	1	5	80
Imitation	40	3	*	5	80

* Less than 1

MIXED DISHES

	Calories Cals.	Total fat Grams	Saturated fat Grams	Cholesterol Milligrams	Sodium Milligrams
Beans, refried (1 cup)	270	3	1	20	1,070
Beef and macaroni (1 cup)	190	6	2	20	970
Beef stew, with vegetables (1 cup)	220	11	4	70	290
Chicken and noodle casserole (1 cup)	370	18	5	100	600
Chicken à la king (1 cup)	470	34	13	220	760
Chicken salad (1/2 cup)	270	25	4	50	200
Chili with beans (1 cup)	290	14	6	40	1,330
Chop suey, beef and pork (1 cup)	300	17	4	70	1,050
Chow mein, chicken (1 cup)	260	11	4	80	720
Coleslaw (1 cup)	80	3	1	10	30
Corned beef hash, canned (1 cup)	380	10	4	130	1,350
Egg salad (1/2 cup)	220	20	4	310	210
Green pepper, stuffed (1)	220	13	5	40	210
Lasagna, with meat (1 piece, 8 oz)	360	18	8	50	720
Macaroni and cheese (1 cup)	430	22	10	20	320
Macaroni salad (1/2 cup)	190	17	3	50	170
Meat loaf, beef (1 piece, 3 oz)	190	12	5	100	390
Moussaka (1 cup)	250	11	4	170	1,320
Pot pie, beef (1 pie, 8 oz)	450	24	6	40	1,290
Potato salad (1 cup)	360	21	4	40	1,090

	Calories Cals.	Total fat Grams	Saturated fat Grams	Cholesterol Milligrams	Sodium Milligrams
Quiche (1 piece, 5 oz)	480	38	18	230	520
Spaghetti and meatballs (1 cup)	330	12	4	90	1,010
Spinach souffle (1 cup)	220	18	7	180	760
Tuna noodle casserole (1 cup)	250	7	2	50	870
Tuna salad (1/2 cup)	190	10	2	10	410

MISCELLANEOUS

	Calories Cals.	Total fat Grams	Saturated fat Grams	Cholesterol Milligrams	Sodium Milligrams
Avocado (1 medium)	310	30	5	0	20
Hummus (1/2 cup)	210	11	2	0	300
Mustard (1 tsp)	5	*	0	0	60
Olives, green (10 olives)	50	6	1	0	940
Peanut butter (1 tbsp)	100	8	1	0	80
Salsa (1/4 cup)	50	3	*	0	110

* Less than 1

FAST FOODS

Fast Foods, Generic (1 regular serving)

	Calories Cals.	Total fat Grams	Saturated fat Grams	Cholesterol Milligrams	Sodium Milligrams
Burrito, beans	320	10	4	20	1,030
Burrito, beef and beans	390	18	7	50	520
Cheeseburger, regular	300	15	7	40	670
Cheeseburger, 4-oz patty	520	31	15	100	1,220
Chicken patty sandwich	440	22	6	70	2,730
Corn dog	330	20	8	40	1,250
Enchilada	240	16	8	20	1,330
English muffin with egg, cheese, bacon	360	18	8	210	830
Fish sandwich	470	27	6	90	620
French fries (3 oz)	270	14	4	10	450
Hamburger, regular	250	11	4	30	460
Hamburger, 4-oz patty	450	21	7	70	760
Hash brown potatoes (3 oz)	190	10	4	0	30
Hot dog	260	15	5	20	750
Hot fudge sundae	310	11	3	20	180
Onion rings (3 oz)	290	16	5	20	490
Pancakes, with butter and syrup (3)	470	10	3	50	1,020
Pizza, cheese (1 slice, 4 oz)	290	9	3	60	700
Pizza, sausage (1 slice, 4 oz)	310	12	4	60	820

	Calories Cals.	Total fat Grams	Saturated fat Grams	Cholesterol Milligrams	Sodium Milligrams
Scrambled eggs (2)	180	15	5	350	230
Taco, beef filling	210	13	5	50	140
Tostada, with refried beans	210	9	4	20	620
Tostada, with beef and beans	330	21	9	60	480
Fast Foods, by Brand Names					
Burger King:					
Whopper	640	41	16	90	840
Whopper, double with cheese	950	60	24	210	1,540
Whopper Junior	370	17	6	40	490
Chicken Sandwich	690	40	11	80	1,420
Chicken Tenders	200	10	3	50	640
Whaler Fish Sandwich	490	27	6	80	590
Kentucky Fried Chicken:					
2-piece chicken dinner					
Original Recipe	660	38	8	170	1,540
Extra Crispy	900	48	12	180	1,530
Biscuit	270	14	4	0	520
Mashed potatoes with gravy	60	1	0	0	300
Coleslaw	100	6	1	5	170
Corn on the cob	180	3	1	0	10
Baked beans	110	1	0	0	390

	Calories Cals.	Total fat Grams	Saturated fat Grams	Cholesterol Milligrams	Sodium Milligrams
Long John Silver's:					
2-piece fish dinner	820	46	11	40	1,580
Seafood Platter	980	58	14	110	2,030
Seafood Salad	430	30	8	80	1,530
Ocean Chef Salad	230	8	2	100	1,900
McDonald's:					
Big Mac	570	35	12	80	980
Quarter Pounder	430	24	9	80	720
McD.L.T.	680	44	15	100	1,030
Filet-O-Fish	440	26	6	50	800
Chicken McNuggets (6)	320	20	5	60	510
English muffin, buttered	190	5	2	20	310
Egg McMuffin	340	16	6	260	890
Sausage McMuffin with egg	520	33	13	290	1,040
Biscuit, plain	330	18	8	10	790
Chef Salad	230	13	6	130	850
Shrimp Salad	100	3	1	190	570
Taco Bell:					
Burrito, bean	360	11	5	10	920
Burrito Supreme	420	19	9	40	950
Taco, regular	180	11	6	30	270
Taco Bellgrande	350	22	13	60	470

	Calories Cals.	Total fat Grams	Saturated fat Grams	Cholesterol Milligrams	Sodium Milligrams
Nachos, regular	360	19	12	10	420
Nachos Bellgrande	720	49	23	40	1,310
Tostada, regular	240	11	5	20	670
Tostada, with beef	320	20	10	40	760
Wendy's:					
Hamburger, Big Classic	470	25	7	80	900
Cheeseburger, double	740	48	18	170	880
Baked Potato, plain	250	*	0	0	60
Baked Potato, with cheese	730	32	20	30	1,370
Chili	260	8	3	30	1,070
Taco Salad	430	19	8	50	1,260

* Less than 1

Dietary Fiber Content
of Common Foods

The following list was compiled from numerous sources, including the latest published data from the U.S. Department of Agriculture, scientific journals, and product manufacturers. Fiber content has been rounded off to the nearest gram for values above 3 grams, and to the nearest one-half gram for lower values.

For a more comprehensive listing, we recommend *Plant Fiber in Foods*, by James Anderson M.D., HCF Nutrition Foundation, P.O. Box 22124, Lexington, Kentucky 40522.

	Calories Cals.	Total fiber Grams	Soluble fiber Grams
Fruits			
Apple, with skin (1 med.)	80	4.0	1.0
Apple, without skin (1 med.)	80	3.0	1.0
Apple juice (1/2 cup)	60	0.5	*
Apple sauce (1/2 cup)	40	2.0	0.5
Apricot, fresh (3 fruits)	50	2.5	1.0
Apricot, dried (5 halves)	40	2.0	0.5
Banana (1 med.)	110	2.0	0.5
Blackberries (1/2 cup)	40	4.0	1.0
Blueberries (1/2 cup)	40	2.5	0.5
Cherries (10 fruits)	50	1.5	0.5
Dates, dried (3 fruits)	70	2.5	0.5
Figs, dried (2 med.)	100	4.0	1.0
Fruit salad (1/2 cup)	60	1.5	*
Grapefruit (1/2 med.)	40	2.0	0.5
Grapefruit juice (1/2 cup)	50	0.5	*
Grapes (20 fruits)	50	1.0	*
Grape juice (1/2 cup)	60	0.5	*
Lemon (1 med.)	20	2.0	0.5
Melon, cantaloupe (1 cup)	30	1.5	0.5
Melon, honeydew (1 cup)	30	1.5	0.5
Nectarine (1 med.)	70	2.0	0.5
Orange (1 med.)	60	2.0	0.5
Orange juice (1/2 cup)	60	0.5	*
Peach (1 med.)	40	2.0	0.5
Pear (1 med.)	70	4.0	1.0
Pineapple (1/2 cup)	40	1.0	*
Plums (3 med.)	40	2.5	1.0
Prunes, canned (1/3 cup)	80	6.0	1.5
Prunes, dried (3 fruits)	60	4.0	1.0
Raisins (1/4 cup)	110	3.0	1.0
Raspberries (1/2 cup)	40	4.0	0.5
Strawberries (1 cup)	50	3.0	1.0
Tangerine (1 med.)	40	2.0	0.5
Watermelon (1 cup)	40	0.5	*

* Less than 0.5

	Calories Cals.	Total fiber Grams	Soluble fiber Grams
Vegetables, Cooked			
Asparagus (1/2 cup)	20	2.0	0.5
Beans, string, green (1/2 cup)	20	2.0	0.5
Beets (1/2 cup)	30	2.0	1.0
Broccoli (1/2 cup)	20	2.0	1.0
Brussels sprouts (1/2 cup)	30	3.0	1.0
Cabbage (1/2 cup)	20	2.0	0.5
Carrots (1/2 cup)	20	2.5	1.0
Cauliflower (1/2 cup)	10	1.5	0.5
Corn (1/2 cup)	90	4.0	1.5
Eggplant (1/2 cup)	20	2.0	1.0
Peas, green (1/2 cup)	60	4.0	1.0
Potato, with skin (1 med.)	100	3.0	1.0
Potato, without skin (1 med.)	100	2.0	1.0
Sauerkraut (1/2 cup)	20	2.0	1.0
Spinach, cooked (1/2 cup)	20	2.0	0.5
Squash, summer (1/2 cup)	20	1.0	*
Squash, winter (1/2 cup)	40	4.0	0.5
Sweet potato (1/2 large)	100	2.0	1.0
Turnip (1/2 cup)	20	2.0	1.0
Zucchini (1/2 cup)	10	3.0	1.5
Vegetables, Raw			
Bean sprouts (1/2 cup)	10	2.0	0.5
Celery, diced (1/2 cup)	10	1.5	0.5
Cucumber (1/2 cup)	10	0.5	*
Lettuce, sliced (1 cup)	10	1.0	*
Mushrooms, sliced (1/2 cup)	10	1.0	*
Onions, sliced (1/2 cup)	30	1.5	0.5
Pepper, green (1/2 cup)	10	1.0	*
Radishes (5 med.)	10	1.0	*
Spinach, raw (1 cup)	10	1.5	0.5
Tomato (1 med.)	20	1.0	*
Tomato juice (1/2 cup)	20	0.5	*
Vegetable juice (1/2 cup)	20	0.5	*

* Less than 0.5

	Calories Cals.	Total fiber Grams	Soluble fiber Grams
Legumes (cooked, 1/2 cup)			
Baked beans	150	9.0	3.0
Black-eye peas	90	10.0	4.0
Dried peas	120	5.0	1.5
Kidney beans	110	6.0	2.5
Lentils	100	3.0	1.0
Lima beans	90	4.0	1.0
Navy beans	110	6.0	2.0
Pinto beans	110	5.0	2.0
Split peas	120	5.0	2.0
White beans	90	5.0	1.5
Baked Products			
Bagel (1 bagel)	150	1.0	*
Bran muffin (1 muffin)	100	3.0	0.5
Corn bread (1 piece):			
Degermed	80	2.0	0.5
Whole ground	80	3.0	1.0
Breads (1 slice):			
Cracked wheat bread	70	1.5	0.5
French bread	80	1.0	0.5
Mixed grain bread	60	1.5	0.5
Oatmeal bread	70	1.0	*
Pita bread (1 pocket)	110	1.0	*
Pumpernickel	80	2.0	1.0
Raisin bread	70	1.0	0.5
Rye bread	70	1.5	0.5
Sourdough	70	1.0	*
White bread	60	1.0	*
Whole-wheat bread	60	2.0	0.5
Crackers:			
Crisp bread (2 crackers)	50	2.0	0.5
Graham (2 squares)	60	3.0	0.5
Saltine (6 crackers)	60	1.0	0.5
Whole wheat (5 crackers)	50	2.0	0.5

* Less than 0.5

	Calories Cals.	Total fiber Grams	Soluble fiber Grams
Breakfast Cereals, Cooked (1 cup)			
Corn grits	150	5.0	1.0
Cream of Wheat	140	3.0	0.5
Oatmeal (rolled oats):			
Regular, quick, or instant	150	4.0	1.5
Whole wheat cereal	150	4.0	1.0
Breakfast Cereals, Ready-to-eat (1 oz)			
40% Bran	90	4.0	1.0
100% Bran	80	10.0	2.0
All Bran	70	10.0	2.0
Bran Buds	70	8.0	1.5
Bran Chex	90	5.0	1.0
Cheerios	110	2.0	0.5
Corn bran	100	6.0	1.5
Corn flakes	110	0.5	*
Cracklin' Oat Bran	110	4.0	1.0
Fiber One	60	12.0	2.0
Fruit & Fiber	100	4.0	1.0
Grape-Nuts	100	3.0	0.5
Granola	130	2.0	0.5
Mueslix	100	4.0	0.5
Nutri-Grain	100	3.0	0.5
Oat bran cereal	100	4.0	1.5
Oat flakes	120	3.0	1.5
Puffed rice	100	0.5	*
Puffed wheat	100	2.0	0.5
Raisin Bran	120	4.0	1.0
Rice Chex	110	1.0	*
Shredded Wheat	100	3.0	0.5
Total (whole wheat)	100	3.0	0.5
Toasted oats	100	3.0	1.5
Wheat Chex	100	3.0	0.5
Wheat germ, plain	110	6.0	1.5
Wheaties	100	3.0	0.5

* Less than 0.5

	Calories Cals.	Total fiber Grams	Soluble fiber Grams
Pasta and Rice (cooked)			
Egg noodles (1 cup)	180	2.5	0.5
Macaroni (1 cup)	140	1.5	*
Rice (1/2 cup):			
Brown	100	3.0	0.5
White	80	1.0	*
Spaghetti (1 cup):			
Whole wheat	160	4.0	0.5
Regular	160	1.0	*
Soups (1 cup)			
Bean soup	120	4.0	1.0
Chicken noodle (or rice)	80	1.0	*
Minestrone	80	3.0	1.0
Onion soup	60	2.0	0.5
Split pea	120	4.0	1.5
Tomato rice	90	1.0	*
Vegetable	70	3.0	1.0
Grains and Flours (dry)			
Barley, pearled (1/2 cup)	300	12.0	3.0
Oat bran (1/2 cup)	120	8.0	4.0
Cornmeal (1/2 cup):			
Whole grain	220	7.0	3.0
Degermed	250	4.0	1.5
Wheat flour (1/2 cup):			
Whole meal	200	7.0	1.5
White, all purpose	210	2.0	0.5
Psyllium supplement (1 tbsp)			3.0
Snacks			
Corn chips (1 oz)	160	1.0	*
Fig bars (2 oz)	210	3.0	0.5
Granola bars (2 oz)	240	1.5	0.5
Oatmeal cookies (2 oz)	250	1.5	0.5

* Less than 0.5

	Calories Cals.	Total fiber Grams	Soluble fiber Grams
Popcorn (2 cups)	60	2.5	*
Potato chips (1 oz)	150	1.5	0.5
Pretzels (1 oz)	120	1.0	*
Tortilla chips (1 oz)	140	2.0	0.5
Nuts (1 oz)			
Almonds	170	4.0	0.5
Brazilnuts	190	2.5	0.5
Cashews	160	2.0	0.5
Filberts (hazelnuts)	180	2.5	0.5
Macadamia	200	1.5	*
Peanuts	160	2.5	*
Pecans	190	2.0	0.5
Pistachio nuts	160	3.0	0.5
Walnuts (black, English)	180	1.5	*

* Less than 0.5

Index